Counselling Theory in Practice

A Student Guide

By Rory Lees-Oakes

Co-Director of CounsellingTutor.com

This book would not have been possible without the patience and dedication of Colette Kelly and the clear insight of Kenneth Kelly. Two of the smartest people I know.

ISBN: 978-0-9957696-2-5

"The soul is healed by being with children."
Fyodor Dostoevsky

For Jacob.

Table of Contents

Foreword xi

Chapter 1   Counselling in the Real World 1

Chapter 2   Choosing Your Course 7
             Counselling and Psychotherapy Courses
             Where to Begin
             Choose a Course which Allows You to Gain
                  Student Membership of an Ethical Body
             Accredited and Non-Accredited Courses
             Degree or Not Degree, That is the Question

Chapter 3   What Modality Should I Study? 27
             Key Differences: Counselling and Psychotherapy
             The Dodo Bird Effect

Chapter 4   Fundamentals of Counselling 35
             Definition of Counselling
             Process of Counselling
             Core Conditions
             Attending to the Client
             Non-Helpful Behaviours

Chapter 5   How Do I Find a Placement? 47
             Don't Try to Blag It!
             Types of Interviews
             Placements and Supervision
             Having Two Placements
             Working with Children

Chapter 6   Making the Most of Your Placement 69
             Importance of Work Experience
             Networking
             Training and CPD
             Supervision
             Staff Committees
             Research Projects
             Policies and Procedure

Chapter 7   Working in a Multidisciplinary Team 75
             Possible Contexts
             History
             Contracting
             Information Sharing
             Guiding Principles

Chapter 8   Assessing Clients 81
             History of Assessment
             Purpose of Assessment
             Areas for Assessment
             Signposting to Other Agencies
             Getting the Timing Right
             Transference and Countertransference
             Use of Assessment Notes
             Risk
             Student Counsellors and Assessment

Chapter 9   Boundaries in Counselling 89
                 Ethical Context
                 Major Boundaries
                 Regular Boundary Issues

Chapter 10   Contracting in Counselling 95
                 Nature of a Counselling Contract
                 Modality of Therapy
                 Number of Sessions Offered
                 Supervision Arrangements
                 Access to Notes
                 Limits of Confidentiality
                 Complaints Procedure
                 Terms and Conditions of Payment
                 Reasons for Counselling Contracts
                 Giving Clients a Copy of the Contract
                 Written versus Verbal Contracts
                 Other Forms of Contracts

Chapter 11   Law in Counselling Contracts 103
                 Contracting
                 Limits to Confidentiality
                 Specific Client Groups

Chapter 12   Reviewing Client Progress 111
                 Pros and Cons
                 Other Modalities
                 Assessment Tools
                 Good Practice in Reviewing
                 Pitfalls in Reviewing

Chapter 13   Stages in Counselling 117
                 Beginning Stage
                 Middle Stage
                 Ending Stage

Chapter 14   The Skill of Attending 123
              Links to Unconditional Positive Regard (UPR)
              Timeline for Attending
              Body Language
              Environmental Factors
              Endings

Chapter 15   Transference in the Therapy Room 129
              What Is Transference?
              Examples of Transference and Counter-Transference
              Warning Signs of Transference in Clients
              Transference in Counsellors
              Struggling to Enter the Client's Frame of Reference
              Experiencing Unrelated Feelings
              Disliking or Over-Liking the Client
              Thinking about the Client between Sessions
              Wanting to Help the Client More than Other Clients
              Looking for an Excuse to Refer a Client On

Chapter 16   Using Timelines in Counselling 137
              Importance of the Past
              How to Use a Timeline in Counselling
              Meaning of the Timeline to the Client
              Proceeding with Caution

Chapter 17   Taking Risks in Therapy 143
              Congruence or Judgement?
              An Example from the World of TA
              Alcohol and Substance Misuse
              Pros and Cons of Taking Risks
              Limiting the Risk

Chapter 18   Making Referrals 147
              Ethical Practice
              Clinical Assessment

Counsellor's Proficiency

Incompatible Personalities

Shared Connections

Client Hesitancy

Relationship Difficulties

Endings

How to Refer

Building Your Knowledge of Agencies

Supervision

Note-Taking

Chapter 19   Trauma-Informed Practice 155

Looking Back

Making Connections

Recent Developments

Examples

Chapter 20   Working Within Your Competence 159

Accepting the Limits of Competence

Feelings of Incompetence

Your Placement

Clinical Supervision

CPD

Limits of Confidentiality

Your Own Process

Don't Be Afraid To Ask

Chapter 21   Working With a Third Person in the Room 165

Examples of Working With a Third Person

Not Ideal, But Still Effective

Choosing an Interpreter

Triangulated Contract

Recording Devices

Debriefing the Interpreter

Lost in Translation?

Cultural Context
Practical Issues

Chapter 22   **Hard-to-Help Clients** **171**
Never Stop Believing
Reasons for Clients Being Hard to Help
Personal History
View of Attachment
Conditions of Worth
Unrealistic Expectations
Social Relationships
Impact of Age
Neurodiversity
Counsellor Process
Keeping Hold of the Lifebelt

Chapter 23   **When Clients Do Not Attend** **177**
Frustrations of DNAs
Attitude is Everything
Common Reasons for DNAs
Other Possible Reasons
Putting a Positive Spin on DNAs

Chapter 24   **Getting Work** **183**

Chapter 25   **Developing Your Internal Supervisor** **191**

Notes **197**

Bibliography **203**

Index **209**

Foreword

I have had the pleasure (and sometimes pain) of knowing Rory in a variety of both professional and personal capacities. I am assuming this is why he requested me to write the foreword for his book. Having known Rory—first as a lecturer, then as a colleague, and now a friend—I feel I have seen the many sides of the man that is Rory Lees-Oakes. I am, therefore, honoured to have been personally asked.

In this book, Rory continues to bring counselling theory to life. This mirrors his prior work in the classroom, where he really offered soil of a different kind for his students to learn and grow. Rory's belief and passion for experiential learning opportunities—the necessary and sufficient conditions being present in the learning environment, teamed with extensive research and understanding of the work of Carl Rogers—all lead to an enhanced education for his students. All this, along with his imaginative use of technology in the classroom, led to his nomination for a Pearson Teaching Award in 2015. This "Silver Plato" award for "Outstanding use of technology in education" marked his retirement from class-based teaching. However, Rory continues to remain dedicated to his work of inspiring counselling learners. Rory has created accessible learning through lectures on the Counselling Study Resource, along with other resources sharing his knowledge and passion.

While both a student, then a colleague of Rory's, I was fortunate enough to witness his faith and determination for his students. His personal moto being, "No one gets left behind", offers autonomy to the student and respects their choice to go as far as they wish on their journey.

Through sometimes lengthy debates, Rory continues to show his thirst for ongoing learning, suggesting new ways to observe or tie the theory in to ever-changing society pressures while maintaining humility to hear others views, experiences, and opinions.

I continue to experience Rory as a man who has a humanistic approach to life, accepting his flaws and successes, striving to continually learn, and becoming all he can be…all while drinking a cup of tea.

I take this opportunity to thank Rory for his faith in the theory, and his patience waiting for essays to be submitted on time and word counts!

– Penelope Russell BSc (Hons) Counselling, MBACP

A Note from the Author

The journey to become a counsellor can be a bit of a bumpy one. You may find yourself experiencing situations for which your counselling course has not prepared you, such as finding a placement, or how to transition from practising skills with a classmate to working with real-life clients in a therapeutic setting.

For example, how would you handle a situation where a client offered you a gift?

Maybe you are taking the first steps in counselling training and are confused about which level to study, or what qualifications are considered appropriate to practice as a counsellor.

Perhaps you have been given conflicting information and you want to get an authoritative answer on questions about which you are unsure.

In this book, you will learn what is the best path to becoming a counsellor and what qualification route may suit your learning style. You will also learn the advantages and disadvantages to consider when choosing a training provider, and practical examples of issues that come up in counselling practice, but are hardly ever covered in an academic textbook or in the classroom.

Are you finding it difficult to gain a counselling placement, in what is becoming a very competitive environment?

Could you use several real-life examples of how to work with common issues which come up time and time again in working with clients?

This book is a direct response to the thousands of questions I have been asked through the years of running our website, counsellingtutor.com, our academic library "The Counselling Study Resource," known as the CSR. I also received many questions from our vibrant Facebook group, which has over 19,000 members at the time of this writing.

One way of responding to the many questions was to run a regular slot on our weekly podcast aptly named *The Counselling Tutor Podcast*, where I answer students' questions which have been sent by email or posted on our Facebook page or website forums.

The podcast is free to download (from iTunes, Spotify or the counselling Tutor website) and is broadcast every week during the academic year with the exception of academic breaks.

Some of my responses from the podcast episodes are reproduced in this book.

I hope to answer your questions and help ease your counselling.

– Rory Lees-Oakes

Chapter 1

Counselling in the Real World

Perhaps one of the greatest challenges for students of counselling and psychotherapy, is crossing the bridge from using counselling skills in a classroom or training setting, to using them in real-world counselling with clients. The main difference is that, in a classroom or training setting, you know your peers and you've probably been with them for a considerable amount of time. More importantly, you and your peers are learning the rules about counselling and psychotherapy. So it's very unlikely that you get any interruptions, or that your counselling skills session would go over time, or that you would get someone who completely shuts down. This is a marked contrast to working with clients in a real world setting. Through my years of supervising student counsellors, I have noticed that a few common themes arise over and over again.

When working with clients, one issue is that the clients may not give you time to do the contracting. They may be so eager to tell their story that all attempts at contracting and introducing your modality of therapy, or discussing how long the sessions last, may get lost as the client starts to talk and outline what's going on with them.

Another issue is that clients may have no sense of time boundaries. In college or with a training provider, it's very likely that when both you and your peer are practising skills, you are sensitive to time. Maybe subconsciously the person who you are listening to will help you out by ending the session on time. However, in the real world of counselling, sometimes clients want to continue telling you about their difficulties, even when the session has ended.

These differences between using skills in a learning classroom setting and using them in a real world scenario can cause students to become anxious, or even lose trust in their abilities. Anne Theriault and Nicola Gazzola described this uncomfortableness as "Feelings of Incompetence", or FOI. They say there is an ongoing struggle for counsellors regarding their level of experience. It is normal to experiencing self-doubt and uncertainty. However, these feelings are often kept hidden, and are not experienced in isolation. Indeed, many counsellors mistakenly believe that they are alone in questioning their own competence. FOI and the taboo around them undermines counsellors' well-being, and insidiously contaminates the therapeutic process. In other words, novice therapists can get tied up in and anxious about how they're using their skills, and if they're getting it right. It may sometimes affect the therapeutic process with clients.[1]

So how do we alleviate the stress and how do we conquer the feelings of incompetence? The first thing to understand is that every student who has made the transition from using skills in a classroom setting to using them in a therapeutic setting with a client has, to some extent, experienced feelings of incompetence, or felt like they were a bit of an imposter. It's also worth noting that all life skills take time to develop. The more you practice, the better you'll become.

There are, however, some particular bridges that students may need to cross. The first of these is wanting to be perfect. So let's clear this off right away: no therapist is perfect. Everybody makes mistakes or, as I like to say, experiences learning opportunities.

I'll give you an example from my own practice. A few years ago, I was summarising the end of a session with a client. As I got to the end, I had a bit of a Eureka moment and realized the summary was not only inaccurate, but it was quite incoherent. I decided, as a matter of congruence, to share this with the client and I asked if she'd like me to summarise again. The client smiled and even laughed a little bit at my nervous apologies and said there was no need to re-summarise, and that we'd meet again next week. When the client returned for the next session, the first thing she said was, "How was your summarising?" I responded by saying that I was hoping it was going to be better than last week's, and would she be kind enough to tell me if that was the case. Reflecting on this event later in supervision, it became apparent that although I'd made a bit of a faux pas in my summary, it had an unintended consequence—it strengthened the therapeutic alliance. Quite simply, my client saw me as a fellow fallible human being—someone who could make a mistake, and admit to it. And if it was okay for me to do that, it was okay for her to do that. Since that day, I invest more time in developing the therapeutic relationship, rather than trying to be a technical expert on skills. I find that the less time I spend overthinking the use of skills, and the more time I spend developing the therapeutic relationship, my skills come more naturally. The skills flow, and were more accurate in the client's frame of reference.

Chapter 2

Choosing Your Course

You are probably already aware of the dizzying array of counselling courses available in the UK. With so many courses to choose from, it's not surprising that one of the questions I am most asked is, "Which qualification path is best?"

When I entered training in 1999, I was faced with quite an array of options, including: the level of qualification; diploma or degree; which modality of therapy to study—Humanistic, psychoanalytical, or cognitive behavioural. There was also a wide range of titles, such as psychiatrist, psychologist, psychotherapist, and counsellor.

In the last nineteen years, I have seen a huge increase in the number of courses that are being offered. I once sat in front of a colleague—a careers adviser at my college—and she literally had her head in her hands as I explained the many routes to becoming a qualified counsellor.

There are many differing routes to helping people who are suffering mental or emotional distress.

The title most people will be familiar with is Psychiatrist.

Psychiatry is a branch of medicine that deals with mental illness or emotional disturbance. To become a psychiatrist, you first need to train as a medical doctor, then take further qualifications in psychiatry. Psychiatry is the study and prevention of mental disorders such as Schizophrenia and Bipolar disorder. Psychiatry also deals with neurological disorders such as brain damage caused by accident, stroke, or degenerative issues such as Alzheimer's and dementia.

According to The Royal College of Psychiatrists, you first need to obtain a medical degree, which takes from four to six years, then undertake further training which could last eight more years.[2]

Psychiatrists can prescribe medication, or admit a patient to the hospital for observation.

This method of helping people is sometimes described as the medical model, based on the idea that mental disturbance is rooted in our biological make up, brain chemistry, or brain structure.

Another title is Psychologist. Psychology is the study of how we think and behave. It's a combination of science-based research and observation of how people behave in certain situations.

Child psychologists help children and parents understand how family dynamics can have an impact on child development, and can provide strategies for families and children to function better and live happier, healthier, emotional lives.

Clinical psychologists help people understand how their behaviour has an impact on their well-being. They may offer treatments such as Cognitive Behavioural Therapy (CBT), or other specific techniques.

The term "clinical" indicates that the person is engaged in helping people with difficulties relating to mental health, or emotional well-being.

The qualification path to becoming a psychologist is to study the subject at degree level, then take further qualifications in a specific area of specialty, such as working with children.

If you are choosing this route, make sure that the curriculum (the subjects taught on the course) support your future ambitions. Psychology degrees can cover a wide range of topics. Some of these topics are not related to the helping professions—for example, a degree in criminal psychology.

Counselling Psychology degrees are the study of how we think and behave, with the added element of practical experience—working therapeutically with individuals in emotional distress.

One of the main differences between a Psychology degree and a Counselling Psychology degree is that the latter includes counselling techniques, skills practice, personal development groups, and theory.

Another major difference is that you will have a clinical placement, regular supervision, and—on qualifying—be able to join a professional body which will allow you to find employment.

Degree courses are usually three years in duration.

At this point, it may be useful to highlight one particular aspect of both psychiatric and psychology training—that of the practitioner being an "expert".

Psychiatrists diagnose and prescribe, psychologists observe and offer interventions. While both disciplines put the client at the centre of the decision-making process, the balance is weighed in the favour of the practitioner.

Counselling and Psychotherapy Courses

The most common question I hear is, *"What's the difference between Counselling and Psychotherapy training?"*

The difficulty in answering this question is that there is no defined definition of either title. One of the ways we can see a difference is in the type of issues counsellors and psychotherapists deal with.

Generally speaking, Counselling tends to be of shorter durations, looking at specific difficulties clients may be encountering, such as self-esteem issues, difficulties in relationships, loss and bereavement.

Psychotherapy is of a longer duration, and tends to be helpful for those individuals who wish to examine their entire life history and make changes.

Psychotherapy courses have a longer duration of training, around 650 training hours, whereas Counselling courses tend to be 450 training hours.

The reason for the longer training duration of psychotherapy courses is that the models of therapy that are taught tend to have a more in-depth theory of personality and, crucially ask the therapist to demonstrate expertise and develop treatment plans.

An example of this would be the theory of Transactional Analysis. As part of the training, therapists are asked to diagnose personality disorders and provide a treatment plan.

Training to be a psychotherapist can take from four to six years. Counselling training equips the individual to be a professional listener, and support individuals who are experiencing life difficulties.

One of the biggest overlaps in counselling and psychotherapy is how the quality of the relationship between therapist and client facilitates change.

At the time of writing this book, there is no legislation or regulation that protects the title of "Counsellor", meaning that there is not one qualification that is seen as a definitive entry into the profession.

Below are answers to frequently asked questions on this subject as well as a statement from the British Association of Counselling and Psychotherapy, one of the lead bodies in counselling and psychotherapy and one that employers look to when recruiting counsellors in the UK.

It also answers the frequently asked question, *"What qualification level must you complete in order to be considered a qualified counsellor?"*

The minimum qualification to be able to be employed, to be accepted into an ethical body such as the BACP and advertise oneself as a qualified counsellor, is a **Level 4 Diploma in Counselling.**

These qualifications are classroom based, and have a minimum of **100 hours supervised placement as an integral part of the course.**

This qualification must be taken with a recognized awarding body, such as **ABC Awards, AIM Awards, CPCAB,** or a University.

Q: I have seen a Diploma in counselling online—is this the same?

A: We are not aware of any "online only" qualification at any level which would allow—on completion—for employment as a counsellor with a reputable service such as the NHS, or allow full membership of an ethical body such as the BACP.

Q: Does a Level 4 Diploma in Counselling allow me to advertise myself as a private practitioner and take on paid client work?

A: Yes, it does.

Q: How do Masters Degrees, PHDs and post graduate qualifications fit in?

A: Some people have already taken higher levels of qualifications in a related subject and may wish to enter training at a higher level, take a more academic route. Universities refer to this as **APL— Accreditation of Prior Learning.**

An example of this would be a graduate with a psychology degree who wishes to train as a counsellor. The university would consider modules taken as part of the degree as APL. In other words, the modules taken on the psychology degree would match the course content of the Master's degree.

Some universities will take students who have completed a Level 3 Certificate or Diploma in counselling skills, providing they are academically capable of completing the course.

Below is a basic guide to counselling qualifications in England, and why people choose a certain route.

Where To Begin?

The first steps to counselling training is to attend a short introductory course that lasts from ten to twelve weeks. These are offered at local colleges or private training providers, and are usually titled *"An Introduction to the Concepts of Counselling"*, or *"Counselling Concepts"*.

These taster courses introduce students to the concepts of counselling, which include a range of counselling theories, equality and diversity, legal and ethical issues, and barriers to communication. Crucially, they also equip students with a basic set of counselling skills which are practiced with peers throughout the course. Part of the program focuses on personal development—the process of linking the theories to our own awareness of how we think, feel, and interact with others.

Engaging with this area of self-awareness is crucially important, as it helps students understand their own barriers or prejudices to being fully present, and being able to listen emphatically (sometimes referred to as walking in another's shoes).

Diplomas Level 4+5 are known as **NVQs (National Vocational Qualifications)** and were designed primarily for people working in jobs who had few, or no qualifications, to be able to evidence competence to their employer, or if changing their job to another employer. The structure of the qualification is observation of skills, practical assessment, and work-based experience with an employer. To pass the qualification, students must complete a portfolio of work showing evidence of competency (recordings, assignments, tutor observation sheets, and employer feedback). There is also an external exam, or in the case of the ABC awarding body, a final submitted portfolio of work.

This qualification route is ideal for those individuals who are coming back to study after an absence from the world of academia. These are students who left school and developed a career outside academia and wish to return to study later in life. It also suits individuals who prefer a less formal style of teaching, with an emphasis on group work and collaborative learning.

The Foundation Degree is sometimes referred to as an Associate's Degree at Level 5. These qualifications focus on specific areas of work and could be viewed as a more academic version of an NVQ, as a large component is evidencing work-based competencies. The duration is usually three years (part-time), or two years (full-time).

This qualification is an ideal "top up" for graduates whose first degree is in a related discipline, such as psychology.

Degrees (BA/BSC) are usually three years in duration, and become more academically challenging as the years progress. The first year is usually at Level 4, the second year at Level 5, and the final year at Level 6. The focus is to explore topics at a more in-depth level, and to produce written work justifying your ideas—including references to books, journals and quality online resources. Learning here is a mixture of group work, formal lectures, with a presented piece of research in the final year. Course structure is a mixture of formal lectures, group work assignments, and a final dissertation.

This qualification is ideal for individuals who want a more in-depth experience of learning and to be tested at a higher level.

Top Up Degree (BA/BSC) is usually taken at a college, but supervised by a university. These are usually one year in duration and cover a number of selected units. Entrance to this qualification is by completing the Diploma Level 4+5. This qualification route is ideal for those who have completed Diploma Level 4+5 and wish to obtain a degree.

Post Graduate Degree, also known as (PGDip, PgDip, PG Dip, PGD, PgD, PDE), is a post graduate qualification awarded after a university degree. The difference is that (unlike a Master's Degree) you are not required to write a dissertation. This is ideal for those who have completed a degree and prefer to study at the same academic level and course structure.

Master's Degree is three years in duration at Level 7. This qualification has research at its heart. The aim of the qualification is considered an area of specialty, and evidence your findings by a final dissertation. Course structure is a mixture of formal lectures, group work assignments, and a final dissertation.

Masters are usually a progression route from a degree. Because of the nature of counselling being an applied subject rather than a dry academic one, there is an element of skill-based observation and reflection on personal development. It is also possible to gain a place on a counselling Master's program with a Level 3 Diploma or Certificate in counselling skills, providing that the university believes that you are academically capable.

PHD or Doctorate (three years) is a research-based endeavour and culminates in a dissertation of approximately 80,000-100,000 words, based on research carried out over the course of the study. The research must be original and create new knowledge in the student-chosen field, or can build on existing knowledge. During the time of study, students will try to get academic papers published and present their work at conferences, which allows them to get feedback on their ideas for their dissertation. At this level, there is very little support from tutors. Students are expected to work independently and will meet their PHD supervising tutor to be assessed on how the research is progressing and if the expected level of academic rigor is being applied.

Usually taken after obtaining a Master's Degree, it is suitable for those who may want to develop their masters research or "plough new ground" in their chosen area of study—building on and developing existing theories or research.

BACP Accredited Courses: The BACP are a leading ethical body for counselling and psychotherapy the UK. As such, course providers (such as colleges and universities) can ask for their courses to be BACP accredited. This means that the course provider has to evidence that the course duration, content, and staffing meet the BACP's specification for course accreditation.

Q: What are the advantages of attending a BACP accredited course?

A: The BACP are providing a seal of quality which some students may find appealing when investing their hard-earned money into training. Also, those who graduate from a BACP accredited course are not required to take the "Certificate of Proficiency" test. Those who graduate from non BACP accredited courses are required to take the test, in order to gain full membership in the BACP.

Before embarking on training and investing huge amounts of time and money, do your research as if you were buying any other product. After all, education is a business. To aid in understanding of this subject, the following is a position statement from the BACP outlining the best practice in training progression route.

We recommend a three-stage training structure.

Stage 1:   Introduction to Counselling
An introductory course will help you gain basic counselling skills and give you an overview of what is involved in counselling/psychotherapist training before you fully commit. These courses are usually offered at Further Education (FE) colleges and adult education centres and last between eight to twelve weeks.

Stage 2:   Certificate in Counselling Skills
This second stage will develop your counselling skills and give you a deeper understanding of counselling theories, ethics, and self-awareness. These courses are usually offered at local FE colleges and adult education centres and are generally one year (part-time). This level of training is also useful for those who do not plan to become counsellors, but whose job involves advising or helping people.

Stage 3:   Diploma in Counselling or Psychotherapy
Your core practitioner training should be at the minimum level of a Diploma in Counselling and Psychotherapy, but could be a degree, masters or doctorate.

To meet the requirements for BACP 2018 membership, this course must be a minimum of one year (full time) or two years (part-time), be classroom-

based, and have at least 100 hours supervised placement as an integral part of the course.

You are not required to take all three stages, but courses have different entry requirements in terms of previous training or experience. For example, if you've been involved in counselling in a previous job, you may be able to start at Stage 2.

If you're unsure, contact a course provider at the appropriate stage and ask about their requirements.[3]

Choose a course which allows you to gain student membership of an ethical body

At the time of this writing, counselling and psychotherapy is not a regulated profession in the UK. This means that anyone can set themselves up in an office, hang a sign on the door saying "Counsellor" or "Psychotherapist", and open for business.

One of the reasons for this is that the terms "counsellor" and "psychotherapist" are not designated titles under the (HCPC) Health & Care Professionals Council—a government-funded regulator of healthcare professionals. The HCPC states:

We are a regulator, and we were set up to protect the public. To do this, we keep a Register of health and care professionals who meet our standards for their training, professional skills, behaviour and health.

– HCPC 2018[4]

Interestingly, some areas or psychology and psychotherapy are deemed "designated titles" under the HCPC. These are:

- Art psychotherapist
- Art therapist
- Drama therapist
- Music therapist
- Practitioner psychologist
- Registered psychologist
- Clinical psychologist
- Counselling psychologist
- Educational psychologist
- Forensic psychologist
- Health psychologist
- Occupational psychologist
- Sport and exercise psychologist

Using any of these titles and practising without being adequately qualified and registered with the HCPC is an offence under Article 39(1) of the Health and Social Work Professions Order 2001, regulated by the HCPC (Health & Care Professionals Council).

So why is counselling and psychotherapy not regulated in the same way? When I qualified in 2004, my tutor reflected that, in time, counselling and psychotherapy would become a regulated profession, but was not sure when that would happen.

During the Blair labour government, the seeds were being sown for regulation. However, progress was slow. After the general election of 2010 lead to a hung parliament, momentum towards regulation stopped and was replaced by the **Professional Standards Authority Accredited Register**—a professional body external of counselling which states:

We are independent and we are accountable to the UK Parliament. Our reports help Parliament monitor and improve the protection of the public. The Health Committee use our performance review reports to question the regulators we oversee about their work. We also encourage organisations to improve the way they register and regulate health and care practitioners in the UK.[5]

There are a number of representative bodies which counsellors and psychotherapist can join—initially as students, and becoming full members upon qualification. These include: the British Association of Counselling and Psychotherapy (BACP), the National Counselling Society (NCS), and the UKCP (UK Counsel for Psychotherapy). All these ethical bodies have their own code of ethics and are recognised under the Professional Standards Authority Accredited Register.

In the absence of regulation, ethical bodies—such as the BACP, UKCP and NCS—have signed up to this register which fulfills two functions. The first function is that it oversees these ethical bodies own disciplinary procedures, and makes them accountable to Parliament.

The second function is to provide a visible quality assurance mark to the general public and a clear path to gaining redress if the service offered has fallen below standard, or a practitioner has transgressed an ethical boundary.

To retain full membership of an ethical body after qualifying, a practitioner must pass a certificate of competence assessment, or complete an accredited course overseen by an ethical body.

If successful, the practitioners are issued a pin number and a logo demonstrating that they are members of The Professional Standards Accredited Register.

Those who go on to the register have to agree that they will abide by the ethical framework, have the relevant indemnity insurance, and undertake at least 30 hours of continual professional development (CPD) per year. There is also a requirement to attend supervision and to respond to any formal complaint made by a client or member of the public.

This system of ethical bodies (being accountable to an organisation who answers to parliament) is a form of regulation, and to some extent, has raised standards and expectations of conduct for those who practice.

Accredited and Non-Accredited Courses

A question I have been asked many times through the years is, *"Is your course accredited?"* After reading this chapter, you will realise that there are many routes to qualifying as a counsellor or psychotherapist—no one qualification is a definite route in to the profession.

So, what is accreditation and how does it work?

As a training provider, you can apply to an ethical body such as the BACP, NCP or UKCP and apply for course accreditation. This means that you pay a fee for representatives of an ethical body to oversee the academic content of the course, staff qualifications, levels of training, and the accommodation where the training takes place.

In 2015, I was asked to support an application by the Manchester Institute for Psychotherapy in their journey to become accredited with the UKCP. The process was a thorough and detailed examination of the organisation which included:

- Staff training levels and experience
- Observation of a lesson
- Review of policies and procedures
- Facilities (building, breakout rooms, accessibility)
- Meetings with the students – past and present
- Integrity of the academic program and taught modules
- Number of training hours

The whole process took approximately six months, and as a result, Manchester Institute for Psychotherapy attained UKCP accreditation.

So, is accreditation a gold standard? It does have some advantages, apart from the ethical bodies seal of approval. Those who take an accredited course are not required to take the ethical bodies certificate of competence test to become full members when they qualify.

And the down side? Gaining accreditations, and keeping them, are two separate things. Accreditation is regularly reviewed and pivots on the training provider—making sure that they abide by the terms and conditions of the ethical body. If for any reason the training provider cannot meet these terms, accreditation is withdrawn.

One of the key elements of being an accredited training provider is that you employ accredited staff members. The difficulty facing colleges and universities is that highly qualified staff are leaving the profession in droves.

One of the consequences of this is that colleges and universities can lose accreditation halfway through the program if their staffing levels do not meet the accreditation threshold. In the current climate of funding cuts in education, it would be wise to considerer the above observations before paying a premium for an accredited course at a government-funded learning establishment.

Degree or not degree, that is the question

"Should I study for a Degree or a Diploma?" is a question I am frequently asked. There is no easy answer to this. You can confidently call yourself a counsellor on passing a Level 4 Diploma in Counselling, run by a recognised body, as discussed earlier in this chapter.

So why would anyone choose to pay more money and spend more time gaining a degree? There are a few advantages to the degree route. The most obvious is gaining the degree, which is a great achievement and is especially gratifying for the majority of students who study counselling and who may be mature "second chancers", returning to education later in life.

Generally, a degree is taken over three years, while a diploma is taken over two years, and at a higher cost.

It is also worth considering that a degree may put you ahead in the employment market, especially if all the candidates interviewed have similar skill sets and personal qualities.

Chapter 3

What Modality Should I Study?

Through the years, I have observed a number of distinct patterns which strongly influence the choice of modality students choose.

Before we explore how these patterns influence choices, it might be useful to explore the roots of the more popular therapeutic approaches taught in the UK and try to answer some of the frequently asked questions on this subject.

The first hurdle is the wide choice of therapeutic approaches that are offered.

John Norcross, Professor of psychology at Scranton University, Pennsylvania, USA, has researched different types of psychotherapy and identified at least 500.[6] In the UK, The British Associations of Counselling and Psychotherapy (BACP) list 31 differing approaches.

Why so many? Well, the answer lies in the term "Paradigm", which finds its roots in the ancient Greek word *paradeiknynai*, meaning "exhibit, represent, or lie side by side". It is also considered a "world view", something everyone can agree on. For example, gravity—we can all agree that if you live on planet earth and drop an object from your hand, gravity will make it fall and hit the ground.

So, let's start with the easy questions first—**Counselling and psychotherapy. What is the difference?**

This question comes up again and again in the counselling tutor Facebook page. Historically in the USA, the term "Psychotherapist" was a protected title and could only be used by those practitioners who had studied and been certified in certain models of therapy, primary Psychoanalysis.

In an article written for the online website *Counselling Resource* author Dr. Greg Mulhauser observes: "It was largely in response to the US prejudice against lay therapists that Carl Rogers adopted the word 'counseling', originally used by social activist Frank Parsons in 1908. As a psychologist, Rogers was not originally permitted by the psychiatry profession to call himself a 'psychotherapist'."[7]

In 1930, when psychologist Carl Rogers proposed his approach "Client Centred Therapy", he referred to it as a "type of psychotherapy".[8]

Key Differences

Counselling: usually a short-term engagement of approximately six to twelve weeks. Clients have a good idea what their issues are, and use the sessions to explore their thoughts and feelings about them. It also encourages them to take positive steps to resolve the difficulties that they are experiencing, or to come to terms with them.

Counselling theories such as "Person-Centred therapy" tend to be less complex, and focus on the quality relationship between therapist and client.

Those who hold counselling qualifications usually train for approximately three years, and qualify with either a diploma or a degree in counselling at level 4 or above.

Psychotherapy: usually a longer-term engagement, which could be up to twelve months or more. The reason for this is that psychotherapy deals with psychological problems which have built up over a lifetime, and may well find their roots in childhood experiences.

Psychotherapy training tends to last from four to seven years, and with those who complete the training gain a level 7 qualification, which equates to a Master's Degree.

Psychotherapeutic theories such a "Transactional Analysis" tend to be theory dense, with a focus on the therapist "teaching" the theory to the client and asking them to apply it to their lives. It should be acknowledged that modern psychotherapy embraces the quality of the therapeutic relationship.

From a client's perspective, if you have a difficulty which you want to explore, make sense of, change, or come to terms with, counselling may help.

If, on the other hand, you want to look at your entire life and make sense of what made you think and act in the world driven by your emotional or mental health, then psychotherapy is probably the way to go.

Simple isn't it? Well, not quite. In the world of counselling and psychotherapy there is no overall agreement as to which approach is the most effective. The reason for this is that human beings are individuals who perceive the world in their own unique way. Throughout the years, theorists and researchers have tried to understand what it is that makes people psychologically troubled, and have come up with a number of theories which are then developed in to therapeutic approaches.

The Dodo Bird Verdict

"The dodo bird effect", was a term coined by Saul Rosenzweig, an American psychologist and therapist who, in 1936, published an article in the *American Journal of Orthopsychiatry* titled "Common Factors in Diverse Psychotherapies". The title is from a well-known race in Lewis Carroll's *Alice in Wonderland*. At the end of the race, the dodo bird observes that those who took part (including Alice) had failed to keep to the race course, so it was impossible to know who won. Declaring, *"everyone has won and all must have prizes."*[9]

Thus, the term "the dodo bird effect" refers to research findings which indicate that there are few or no meaningful differences between the different approaches in counselling and psychotherapy. Positive outcomes seem to pivot on the quality of the therapeutic relationship, which boils down to how much trust the client has in the therapist.

 Go to https://counsellingtutor.com/024-choosing-your-modality-irrational-thoughts/ for a Podcast on this topic.

The first theorist to do this was the Austrian scientist Sigmund Freud, who in the late 1800s developed an approach called **Psychoanalysis** later referred to as "The first force in psychology".

Freud hypothesised that events in childhood had a significant influence on our adult lives, which influenced personality traits. A traumatic event in a child's past may result in the memory being hidden from consciousness, which causes problems during adulthood (in the form of anxiety or, as Freud termed it, Neurosis).

Psychoanalysis is still taught and practised today. It has influenced other approaches, in particular Transactional Analysis, which developed on Freud's theory of subconscious process and childhood messages being played out in adulthood.

"*The second force in psychology*" rose in America during the 1920s and 1930s, and developed theorists like Edward Thorndike, Fredrick Skinner, and John Watson who trained animals to open boxes and pull leavers to gain rewards of food. This approach became known as behaviourism.

Behaviourism: the idea that behaviour could be modified through the use of punishment and reward to alter how we thought or behaved.

Behaviourism is still used today. If you drive down the road and see a speed camera, you are likely to slow down. The reason for this is that you fear the "punishment" of a speeding ticket—this influence how you think about your speed.

Behaviourism influenced Cognitive Behavioural Therapy in that it sees modifying or changing behaviour as a way of managing or changing psychological states, such as anxiety or depression. It is often used to treat eating disorders.

"*The third force in psychology*", a term coined by Abraham Maslow, are humanistic therapies of which **Person-Centred Therapy** is perhaps the best known. The term 'Humanistic' was used to indicate a shift away from Psychoanalysis which focused on subconscious and biological drives and Behaviourism, which considered an individual's behaviour could be 'conditioned' or 'programmed' through the use of punishment and reward.

Humanistic therapies can trace their roots to a philosophical idea known as Phenomenology, the study of individual perceptions. Humanistic therapies focus on an individual's world view and how that is distorted or rejected by those close to them.

The terms' introjected values and conditions of worth speak of individuals having to reshape their concept of self to fit in with others expectations. The basis of humanistic therapies is to help a person work out what they want and not live to others' expectations.

Chapter 4

Fundamentals of Counselling

Definition of Counselling

In their book *Dictionary of Counselling* (Wiley, 2004, p. 53), Colin Feltham and Windy Dryden define counselling as:

> *A principled relationship characterised by the application of one or more psychological theories and a recognised set of communication skills, modified by experience, intuition and other interpersonal factors, to clients' intimate concerns, problems or aspirations. Its predominant ethos is one of facilitation rather than of advice-giving or coercion. It may be of very brief or long duration, take place in an organisational or private practice setting and may or may not overlap with practical, medical and other matters of personal welfare.*

> *It is both a distinctive activity undertaken by people agreeing to occupy the roles of counsellor and client and it is an emergent profession. It is a service sought by people in distress or in some degree of confusion who wish to discuss and resolve these in a relationship which is more disciplined and confidential than friendship, and perhaps less stigmatising than helping relationships offered in traditional medical or psychiatric settings.*[10]

This quote differentiates counselling from other helping activities, such as being a friend or offering medical advice. It also makes it clear that those who attend counselling should do so in the full knowledge that this is what they are engaging in. Indeed, it would be deemed unethical (and may be damaging) to actively counsel a person who did not specifically intend to enter therapy, and who did not fully understand the limits of confidentiality and the number of sessions available.

Process of Counselling

For the client, counselling is centred on the difficulties that they are experiencing. To some extent, it provides a learning situation where the client can gain insights into their behaviour and how they relate to others. As this process unfolds, they can choose what they wish to change, or find ways by which to accept. A key aspect of counselling relies on the client's motivation and readiness to change, and on the level of trust and the depth of the therapeutic relationship with the counsellor.

As for the therapist, there are various healthy and ethical behaviours and mechanisms that the counsellor may adopt in order to offer the best possible service to their clients.

Seeing the Client as an Individual

Counselling.can be defined as a "permissive relationship"—that is, the client has permission to say what they want without being reprimanded or judged.

Each client and their decision-making process must be fully accepted. This does not mean that the counsellor has to approve of all their behaviour, but that they need to accept the client themselves as a person of worth. Counselling helps clients to reach their own decisions.

Creating the Right Relationship

For any meaningful therapeutic work to take place, it is imperative that the counsellor pays attention to the ebb and flow of the relationship between themselves and the client. There are many differing models of how to build and sustain a meaningful therapeutic relationship.

One of the most well-known models was developed by American psychologist Carl Ransom Rogers, who first published his model in the *Journal of Consulting Psychology* in 1957 (pp.95–96) in the USA. There, he proposed six "necessary and sufficient conditions of therapeutic personality change":[11]

> *For constructive personality change to occur, it is necessary that these conditions exist and continue over a period of time:*
>
> 1. *Two persons are in psychological contact.*
> 2. *The first, whom we shall term the client, is in a state of incongruence, being vulnerable or anxious.*
> 3. *The second person, whom we shall term the therapist, is congruent or integrated in the relationship.*
> 4. *The therapist experiences unconditional positive regard for the client.*
> 5. *The therapist experiences an empathic*

understanding of the client's internal frame of reference and endeavors to communicate this experience to the client.

6. *The communication to the client of the therapist's empathic understanding and unconditional positive regard is to a minimal degree achieved.*

Condition 1: Two Persons Are in Psychological Contact

Right from the start of the relationship, it is important for the therapist to assess whether the client shares the same reality as themselves. This may not be so if the client presents under the influence of alcohol or drugs, or in a psychotic state. Either of these scenarios would mean that therapy would not likely be effective, as it is hard—or even impossible—to enter a frame of reference that is distorted or disconnected.

Condition 2: The First, Whom We Shall Term the Client, Is in a State of Incongruence, Being Vulnerable or Anxious

This condition raises the question of whether it is possible to counsel someone who does not have any difficulties they wish to explore. Like condition 1, this is very much an assessment condition that the therapist may use to ascertain whether the client has accessed the right form of helping.

Condition 3: The Second Person, Whom We Shall Term the Therapist, is Congruent or Integrated in the Relationship

This condition is the first of what is referred to as the "core condition". In terms of effective helping, this condition asks the counsellor to be their real and genuine self in the relationship, sometimes referred to as being "congruent".

Condition 4: The Therapist Experiences Unconditional Positive Regard for the Client

The second of the core conditions asks the counsellor to be non-judgemental and accepting of the client. This requires the counsellor to accept the client—not necessarily their behaviour. In other words, we must separate the sin from the sinner. This is not always easy, but the healing power of non-judgement is enormous: the freedom to speak about issues that are surrounded in guilt, shame or fear in a non-judgemental atmosphere can be hugely therapeutic.

Condition 5: The Therapist Experiences an Empathic Understanding of the Client's Internal Frame of Reference and Endeavors to Communicate This Experience to the Client

This—the third (and last) core condition—speaks of the counsellor's empathy in response to the client. The ability for the counsellor to enter the client's frame of reference and to experience the client's experiences with all the attendant thoughts and feelings allows the client to feel both heard and understood. For some clients this may be a new and powerful experience—possibly the first time in their entire life that someone has really tried to understand them.

Condition 6: The Communication to the Client of the Therapist's Empathic Understanding and Unconditional Positive Regard is to a Minimal Degree Achieved

This final condition is about how the client feels about the counsellor. The client may initially ask themselves whether they can trust the counsellor with their secrets, shame and fear. If the counsellor—by demonstrating empathy, congruence and UPR—can convince the client that they care, then the process of building a therapeutic relationship can proceed.

Core Conditions

We can think about the core conditions as the "care" conditions. In other words, if the client feels cared for, this opens up the possibility for them to explore all the difficulties and emotions they are experiencing. This can allow the client to achieve considerable growth.

In fact, Rogers himself never used the term "core conditions". In an article entitled "The case of the lost conditions", published in the February 2000 edition (p. 34) of *Counsellor* (a forerunner to *Therapy Today*), Keith Tudor explains:

> The term "core conditions" seems to have been coined by Carkhuff... who used it in the context of identifying from divergent orientations to therapy "core, facilitative and action-oriented conditions" by which the helper facilitated change in the client (or "helpee"). In addition to empathic understanding, respect and genuineness, these included: specificity in emphasising emotional experiencing, concreteness in problem-solving, the ability to confront and the ability to interpret the helping relationship.[12]

Robert Carkhuff was a student of Rogers; he was keen to apply empathy, congruence and UPR to other helping roles, such as his own profession of social work. The idea stuck, meaning that most helping professions now use the core conditions of empathy, congruence and UPR as a basis for building positive helping relationships.

Attending to the Client

One of the most useful models of helping behaviour was developed by Gerard Egan, Professor Emeritus of Loyola University of Chicago, USA, and outlined in his book *The Skilled Helper* (originally published in 1975 by Wadsworth). There, he set the baseline for listening and demonstrating to the client that they have your full attention, using the acronym "SOLER":[13]

- S (Squarely): Sit squarely facing the client, to show that you are present and paying attention.
- O (Open): Keep an open posture, not crossing your arms and legs, to help the client feel engaged and welcome.
- L (Lean): Lean forward when the client speaks to you, to show that you are involved and listening to what they have to say.
- E (Eye): Use good eye contact, to indicate that you are listening and not distracted (though it's important to bear in mind that eye contact can be seen as less positive in Eastern cultures).
- R (Relaxed): Try to be reasonably relaxed, staying calm and avoiding fidgeting, to show that you are focused on what the client is saying.

The use of these techniques has been adopted all over the world by helping professionals such as counsellors, nurses and social workers who wish to demonstrate they are giving their full attention to the client.

Non-Helpful Behaviours

As in all professions, there are potential pitfalls in counselling. Some types of interventions—especially those that we could describe as counsellor-centred rather than client-centred—are unhelpful and can leave the client feeling judged or spoken down to. In the following sections, I discuss some of the most common mistakes by new counsellors.

Advice-Giving
Any conversation that begins "If I were you …" gives the impression that you know the client better than they know themselves. The whole point of counselling is to help the client to find their own answers and to make sense of what is going on in their life.

Lecturing
Imagine being a client speaking about a relationship break-up and your counsellor responds: "Well, you should have tried harder. It seems to me that you were not giving her enough attention, which is why she went off with someone else. Have you thought of losing weight and finding a good hairstylist?" I doubt you would want to return for another session—or even to finish the one you were in! Lecturing a client is the worst type of judgement and can leave you feeling that it's all your fault and that you are not good enough.

Excessive Questioning
As a client, if your counsellor keeps asking question after question, and seems better suited to a career as an interrogator, you know you are in trouble! Excessive questioning can feel intrusive to the client, and give them the impression that the counsellor is either very nosy or is having trouble believing the client. Either way, it may feel like a police interview rather than therapy.

Storytelling

It's also important never to start your response with the words: "The same thing happened to me ..." Like advice-giving, storytelling comes from the teller's frame of reference and has nothing at all to with the client's experiences or feelings. The client could feel ignored and discounted—and even end up knowing more about you than you know about them!

Asking "Why?"

On the face it, "Why did you do that?" may seem a reasonable question to ask, but in fact it transmits a form of judgement, and may even take the client back to their childhood or school days—in other words, to a time when they were required to justify themselves by those in authority.

If you need to help understand the client's motivation, a better response might be: "What was it that made you do that, do you think?" This is an adult-to-adult question that is value-free, as it passes no intrinsic judgement.

Asking "How Did That Make You Feel?"

This response is a real counselling cliché, which may therefore come across as rather patronising and shallow. Of course, it's important to try to get a sense of how their clients feel about any given situation by asking an appropriate question, but this needs to be done sensitively and with care. One useful way to express this might be: "I'm curious to understand the feelings you have around this". This could be a good way of invoking a thoughtful response from the client.

Rescuing

Suppose that a counsellor says to their client: "If you need me, ring at any time of the day or night" or "Would you like me to speak with your boss who is bullying you?" In these cases, the counsellor would have crossed a very definite boundary, and would in effect be depowering the client. Rescuing gives the impression that a client does not have their own agency and is dependent on the therapist.

Chapter 5

How Do I Find A Placement?

To gain full membership of an ethical body such as the British Association of Counselling and Psychotherapy (BACP), The National Counselling Society (NCS), or the UK Counsel for Psychotherapy, you need to be studying at UK Level 4 or above and have face-to-face training—not online (see the chapter Choosing My Course).

Reputable counselling courses ask learners to undertake a minimum of one hundred hours of supervised client work as part of their training. This includes finding a placement in an organisation which offers a counselling service where students can gain training experience.

For most students, this causes great anxiety, as they must write, email, phone, and turn up to organisations to try to get a placement. This can leave learners downhearted at being rejected, and sometimes a little paranoid that they won't get a placement.

A few years ago, I was sitting in the reception of the charity I worked with, waiting for a client, when a young man walked in and asked a member of the staff, "Do you have any counselling placements?" The answer was an emphatic "No".

Unfortunately for him, he was speaking to the cleaner who had as much idea on counselling placements as I have about astrophysics! Consequently, he was left with no placement, and a bit down in the dumps. The moral of the story: find out who you are talking to and what their role is in the organisation!

In this section, we are going to look at strategies for gaining a placement, and ways of making sure that your application gets seen in a favourable light.

1. You are Applying for a Job

Charities (sometimes referred to as "The third sector") are a sophisticated business that relies on financial support from the public and "principle donors" such as local or national government, the business world, and the European Union funding (EEC).

As such, they want volunteers who will uphold the principles of the organisation and add value to the business, giving confidence to the general public and the funders.

If all this seems a little harsh, welcome to reality. Charities are businesses—so your application and interview need to be professional.

2. Check Your Values

I have interviewed numerous students for placements, and there is nothing worse than knowing that the person sitting in front of you has no interest in the organisation or its values—they just need a placement—any placement.

Before applying to an organisation, consider if their values and client group are of interest to you. Do you believe that you could really make a difference in their clients' lives?

Counselling is about being honest and ethical. As a student, I turned down a placement working with aged people because of events in my life. Where I was as a person at the time led me to believe that perhaps I could not give my all to the client group.

If you do not have a valid reason to apply to the organisation (other than you need a placement), then you are wasting their time and yours.

3. Contact the Person Who Makes the Decisions

Find out the principal person responsible for placements. They usually have the title "volunteer co-coordinator", or "practice manager" (which I will now refer to as the "principle"). You can do this by looking on the website of the organisation, or phone to confirm. Make sure you get the person's email address, work phone number, and mailing address. At this point, you don't need to talk to the principle, you just need to confirm their name and contact details.

4. Do Your Homework

As discussed in part one, charities are a business and as such, there is an expectation that you will know about them, what they stand for, and what they do.

Bear in mind that you are not going for an interview for a commercial position. Knowing the annual turnover, staff ratios and funding streams may sound impressive, but you are applying for a counselling placement—you may be a bit wide of the mark.

Instead, focus on issues that are relevant to your application, such as the impact the charity has on the local community, its reputation with your peers on the course, the client group they work with, and any positive feedback you have heard locally or from friends and family who have used the service. Be thoughtful of confidentiality — don't mention names or specific situations.

Also, discuss any fundraising initiatives that caught your eye. One student I interviewed a few years ago thought it was funny that the charity I worked with had turned part of Supermarkets Car Park into a tropical paradise which included a beach, palm trees, and our volunteers dressed in Hawaiian shirts offering non-alcoholic cocktails to bemused shoppers.

The conversation which followed demonstrated to myself and the rest of the interview panel that she really understood the ethos and values of the organisation.

That kind of interaction at an interview can really make a difference.

5. Have a Smart Approach

Practice managers are inundated with enquiries from prospective student counsellors, phone calls, emails, and people turning up without an appointment. Most will not admit it publicly, but students can sometimes be a bit distracting to their work.

So you need to be smart.

In part 3 we discussed finding the principle, and if you have followed the instructions, you will have:

- The person's name
- Their email address
- Their phone number
- And a mailing address

Contact by phone is the easiest, but is the least productive. Most practice managers work part-time, and spend their working day with clients, meetings or client assessments. They will not be sitting by the phone waiting for you to call. But if you do reach them by phone, they will probably be between meetings and have very little time to talk.

So we are going to use an old-fashioned, tried-and-tested method of communication—the humble letter. I will explain why later.

The secret of good communication is to impart as much information in the shortest possible time.

22 New Bank Gardens
Bridge Town
BL3 4NM
3rd of February 2013

Dear Ms Davis,

I am a Counselling Diploma student in my first year of a two-year level 4 program at Bridge Town College. My reason for writing to you is to inquire when you will be interviewing for counselling placements.

I am a Student Member of the BACP, have indemnity insurance from AXIA, and have been passed as "fit to practice" by my college tutor, Rory Lees-Oakes, who will provide a letter to that effect.

Last year, I obtained my level 3 certificate in counselling skills at Bridge Town, having completed the level 2 the previous year.

I am attracted to your organisation because (Give valid and honest reasons—in this section you could include any relevant work or volunteering experience if applicable).

I can be available at short notice, as I live 10 minutes away by car and can be contacted at the above address or by email at Jmills@ powermail.co.uk. My mobile number is 07777 7777.

I look forward to hearing from you.

Yours sincerely

Jenny Mills

In this letter you have answered most questions the principle would initially want to know. In four paragraphs, you have shared the following valuable information:

- Your course, course level, previous qualifications, college, and tutor
- Professional obligations (such as membership of the BACP, and insurance)
- The fact that you are passed and ready for practice, and can evidence this
- What attracts you to the organisation
- Previous experience (if applicable)
- Availability and locality to the organisation

The reason for writing a letter initially is that letters are hard to ignore, they hang around the principles' desk, and if you use good quality paper and envelope, your letter will demand immediate attention.

The next stage of contact is to send an email, a week later (if you have not heard anything in the meantime) which reads like this:

To: Vdavis@charityone.co.uk
From: Jmills@powermail.co.uk

Re: my letter

Dear Ms Davis,

Please excuse my email so soon after I have written to you. I thought you may find it useful to have a return email address.

Kind regards

Jenny Mills

What you have done here is to raise awareness of your letter. if it was not received, or got stuck in the post room, then the principle will go and find it or email you to ask what it was about.

If she has received your letter, then it might trigger a quick response by email. Notice how the email is "reader centred" ("I thought you might find it useful"). This technique makes it easier for the person to respond.

Between the letter and the email, you have made the practice manager's life easier—they get lots of enquiries from prospective placement counsellors.

You have supplied valuable decision-making information in your letter and a fast method of response in your email.

If you don't get a follow up, give it another week and then phone the organisation to see if the principle is still working there, or is on extended leave. If it is the latter, find out who is covering the work and repeat the steps outlined in part three.

Finally, remember the old adage, "a squeaking hinge gets oiled first". In other words, be persistent but in a respectful and constructive way.

6.   Other Routes to Placements

Bearing in mind my earlier comments on values, some students volunteer for an organisation before they enter counselling training. This has many advantages—such as giving back to your community, and making a difference to individuals who may have had (or are having) difficulties in their lives.

One of the main advantages of volunteering early is that you can see how the organisation works, what its values are, and you can meet other colleagues who may prove useful future contacts.

When counselling placements are available, you will have a good understanding of the organisation, plus you will know the people interviewing you.

7. Preparing for an Interview

In my experience both as a student and tutor, one of the greatest sources of student angst is gaining a placement—especially if your peers are getting into practice, and you are still waiting to start.

The self-inflicted pressure that some students go through can be quite destructive, which in turn leads to a fantasy of having the perfect interview—and the associated stress that comes with it.

In this section, we are looking to swap stress for knowledge and competence, which will lead to obtaining your goal of a placement. We will also look at things such as interview structures, dress codes, and questions you will likely be asked.

a. Don't Try to Blag it!

The individuals on an interview panel will be counsellors who are involved in counselling at some level. Consequently, they will be a good judge of character and will be able to tell if you are not being truthful.

If you don't know the answer to a question, say "*I don't know*", which is the wisest answer you can give and tells the interviewer two important things: that you are honest; and that you have the confidence to be honest.

Types of Interviews

Group Interview

In this scenario, you will be placed in a group and given a question to answer relevant to counselling, such as confidentiality or an ethical dilemma such as, "Is touch appropriate in counselling?"

What the interviewers are looking for is how you interact with others. Are you co-operative or defensive? Do you value others' opinions, even if they are different from your own? Can you work as part of a team and challenge appropriately?

In the group interview I attended for my diploma course, we were asked, "when would you break confidentiality?" As we were debating, one member of the group started wagging his finger at another stating in a loud voice, "I have a big problem with that." Needless to say, he did not get a place on the course.

Individual Interview

This is where you usually sit in front of a panel of interviewers (usually three) who will ask you questions similar to the following:

- What attracts you to the organisation?
- What course and college are you attending?
- Your availability—how much time can you offer the organisation?

- A question about confidentiality or ethics
- A question on equality and diversity
- A question about managing confidentiality with a client who self-harms or may be feeling suicidal
- A question on self-care—how do you look after yourself? What do you do outside of counselling?
- Questions about your strengths and weaknesses
- Questions you would like to ask about the organisation

They may ask you if have you any questions for the panel. Responses such as, "How many counsellors work here?" and, "Do you have different modalities of therapy available?" are thoughtful answers and demonstrate you have a wider interest in the organisation outside of getting a placement.

At the end of the interview, they may ask for a "fitness to practice" letter, sometimes known as a "letter of comfort", which is written to the organisation from your tutor on letterhead, stating that in his or her opinion you are ready to work with clients.

You will probably be told that the organisation will be in touch. You can ask for feedback—remember you can learn more from a defeat than a victory.

It has to be said that not all organisations interview like this. But as I always say to my learners, "Hope for the best—Prepare for the worst."

As discussed earlier, charities are business-minded and want those who work with them to reflect the ethos and values of the organisation, as experienced by both the public and stakeholders, which is another word for funders.

b. Dress Code

Smart casual is the order of the day; don't turn up dressed for a night out or a day on the beach. The way employees at the organisation dress will be the dress code, so let that guide you. Remember, interviewers will be trying to assess how you will come across to clients, and the way you dress will be a good indicator.

Avoid suits or uniforms — if you have to wear either of these at your day job and you are going straight from work, my advice would be to change before the interview.

8. Timing is Important

One of the reasons students struggle to find placements is timing. When looking to recruit placement counsellors, most agencies or charities work with the academic calendar of colleges and universities. The academic year starts in September for further education colleges, and in October for universities. Most placement providers work to the theory that within twelve weeks students have had their skills assessed and have been signed off by their tutors as fit to practice.

This usually is conducted in a formal way with students being assessed and tutor feedback given. At the end of this process, students are sometimes issued a "fitness to practice" letter, which they take to their placement interview as a way of assuring placement providers they are ready to work with clients.

The outcome of this process is that placement providers usually start their recruitment cycles in December or January, safe in the knowledge that they will have a large cohort of ready-to-go students to choose from.

The other crucial time is in June or July. The reason for this is that when students graduate in June, some leave their placement, which provides a vacancy.

Understanding the supply and demand cycle of placement providers is a good way of being successful and securing valuable face-to-face client work.

9. If it Sounds Too Good to be True, it Usually is
Through the years, I have lost count of the number of students who came to me with "*a dream placement*".

When examined, this dream was actually a nightmare of ethical and moral issues. Let me explain.

Most UK awarding bodies such as ABC Awards, CPCAB and university courses have clear guidelines as to what constitutes a suitable placement for the student therapist. The reason for this is that students need to be supported in their placement and work with clients within their **range of experience**.

Some Examples of Dreams and Nightmares

One charity working with homeless men decided to save money by dispensing with the services of a paid, qualified, experienced counsellor and use students instead. They considered it appropriate to have a non-qualified receptionist assess clients for counselling. The difficulty here is that without proper assessment, a novice therapist may find them working with issues beyond their skill set or experience.

The second issue was that the charity only had a handful of clients. This meant that there was a possibility that the student counsellor could run out of clients. Added to this was the transitory nature of the client group (moving on, getting rehoused) so there was a strong possibility that any engagement in therapy was going to be of very short duration. The possible impact of this was that the student would not experience sufficient sessions to understand and crucially experience the process of therapy, which led to another difficulty of not being able to write a case study. Do you see what I mean about a nightmare?

Another example was a student whose company offered her a placement. On further investigation, it transpired that the "role" was to offer colleagues being made redundant as part of a restructure counselling—some of whom she worked with. Do you see what I mean by ethical and moral issues?

It is for reasons like these that awarding bodes have guidelines in place to help students get the right experience as they begin their practice journey.

An example of these guidelines can be found in the specification documents of awarding bodies and university guidelines. Below is the advice taken from the CPCAB awarding body specifications: (*current at the time of this writing*)

> *Tutors need to ensure that candidates are in safe, ethical, and well-managed agencies or placements:*
>
> - *The placement must offer candidates the opportunity to demonstrate their proficiency in the relevant assessment criteria and at the relevant service level.*
> - *The quality and depth of experience offered in the workplace needs to match the training, ability, proficiency and experience of the candidate.*
> - *Client experience should not be limited to a narrow client group unless there is a descriptor (e.g. working with young people) attached to the qualification (and even in this case candidates still have to meet all the generic criteria of the qualification).*
>
> *Agency/Placement Responsibilities*
>
> - *To offer formal induction to volunteers/trainee counsellors*

- *To make volunteers/trainee counsellors aware of all relevant agency policies and procedures including:*
  - *code of conduct, complaints and health and safety procedures*
  - *confidential handling of client records according to agency policy and data protection law*
  - *to clarify agency training requirements for volunteers/trainee counsellors*
  - *to clarify administrative procedures*
  - *undergoing a CRB check (if required)*
- *To set out an agreed, explicit referral procedure*
- *To take clinical responsibility for the client work*
- *To carry out prior assessment of clients or assist the volunteers/trainee counsellors in carrying out client assessments*
- *To provide a safe therapeutic space for the counselling work*
- *To clarify relevant expense arrangements (e.g. travel costs, supervision costs)*
- *To give written feedback to the volunteers/ trainee counsellors to meet course requirements*
- *To receive or send a "cause for concern" report (if required)*
- *To attend a "cause for concern" meeting at the college/centre (if required)*

As you can see, choosing the right placement is more than just putting in your hours—it is about being supported, nurtured, and developed as an emerging practitioner.

Placements and Supervision

Your placements will have differing requirements for supervision. Some will be satisfied with your external supervision arrangements and ratios, while others will expect you to attend in-house supervision as well.

Group supervision can add a different dynamic to your learning and as a bonus, some awarding bodies will allow you to claim it against your required supervised hours.

There is another form of placement supervision which has emerged over that the last few years. This is where you agree to in-house supervision as part of being offered a placement. This means that you pay the placement to be supervised. This type of arrangement needs careful consideration of:

- Not being able to choose a supervisor who fits you and your needs
- What happens if you feel yourself and the supervisor don't work well together?
- How free are you to criticise the organisation if you are being supervised by them?
- How do you gauge value for money?

You can, of course, pay for external supervision. However, this brings its own difficulties, such as having to pay twice, conflict of advice or direction (one supervisor may tell you to work one way with a client, the other supervisor may contradict this)—whose direction do you choose? What happens if you gain another placement? Will your in-house supervisor supervise your other work?

Finally, most academic institutions ask your supervisor to write a report at 50 or 100 hours. Who writes it? Your in-house supervisor, or your external supervisor?

If you are thinking of a placement with tied supervision, be sure that it can cover all of your practice hours as required by the course. Also, speak to students who are already at the placement ask them about their experiences before you make a decision.

Having Two Placements

Some students take on a second placement, which can help increase your counselling hours. This is especially useful if you have several no-shows or DNAs (Did Not Attend). It is also a great opportunity to work with a different client group and a new organisation.

When considering taking on another placement, it is worth considering the following points:

- How many clients will your training provider allow you to have per week?
- How much extra supervision will you need?
- If you have compulsory supervision at one placement, will they supervisee you for another placement?
- If the answer to the above question is no, you will have to find a separate supervisor.
- If you have two supervisors, who will write your supervision report?

Generally speaking, taking on another placement is only advisable if you have an external supervisor and they are willing to supervise all your client work.

Also consider that each of the placements will want 100% of your commitment. Before taking on a second placement, it may be useful to speak with your tutor and supervisor.

Working With Children
You may want to work with children. Before walking this path, there are a few things you need to consider.

- Most awarding bodies limit you to having only 50% of your hours with children, which means that you will need to have two placements.
- Awarding bodies have strict requirements in terms of working with children.

The awarding body Centra, known as ABC, state the following in their 2018 counselling specifications:

> *Young People / Young Persons are those aged 13 – 17 inclusive that are undergoing counselling. Centres are strongly advised to discourage trainees from working with young people (and also with 18 year olds or those who turn 18 during the course of the placement activity, or with vulnerable adults) unless they have received formal training and can demonstrate that they are conversant with current legislation and organisational, local and national policies. If trainees wish to include client hours with young people it is anticipated that they will have had at least 3 years' experience of working in a professional supportive capacity with this age group. Centres need to be satisfied that trainees have the required experience*

and should ask them to produce proof of their experience.[14]

Another well-respected awarding body, CPCAB, states:

> *Courses are not all the same. The CPCAB level 4 Diploma is assessed to a national standard via a common set of learning outcomes and associated assessment criteria, but each individual centre has its own unique training programme. If the centre training programme (1) includes specific skills and knowledge for working with children and (2) the tutors are themselves suitably qualified and experienced in this area, they may support candidates to take up placements working with children.*
>
> *If the course itself does not include specialised training for working with children but the agency offers and supports candidates to work with children via their own induction and training programmes, candidates may undertake a proportion of their hours with children, provided the course tutors are happy to support this.*
>
> *In all cases, candidates should be supported by appropriate clinical supervision. This is often provided by the agency itself.*[15]

As the above specifications outline, working with children requires special skills and knowledge, especially in the area of child protection and the law.

There is also another consideration: most models of therapy such as Person-Centred Therapy and Cognitive Behavioural Therapy were developed primarily for adults and are possibly not very effective with younger children.

At some point you will be asked to "map" the theory to a case study. This could be very difficult if you are working with very young children, because they have a very different world view than adults. This is because they generally lack life experience, and their cognitive processes are yet to mature—an observation highlighted by the French Philosopher, Maurice Merleau-Ponty, who observed that children have a differing form of phenomenological experience to adults.

He observed:

> The perception of other people and the intersubjective world is problematic only for adults. The child lives in a world which he unhesitatingly believes accessible to all around him. He has no awares of himself or of others as private subjectives, nor does he suspect that all of us, himself included, are limited to one certain point of view of the world.[16]

Chapter 6

Making the Most of Your Placement

Importance of Work Experience

If you decide to progress onto a diploma or maybe a degree in counselling, the course curriculum will ask you for some work experience. Certainly, this is the case in the UK. This takes the form of a placement, which provides the opportunity for you to work with clients and gain experience.

Having a counselling placement is important not only to gather the required hours of experience in working with real clients, but also to gain other types of professional development (which may be useful for a future career). For example, you can build contacts and resources that may help you when you graduate and begin to seek work as a qualified counsellor. This chapter offers useful tips to help you make the most of your placement.

Networking

It's important to take the opportunity to network with other therapists and staff at the placement. You'll be amazed at the knowledge you can gain over a cup of coffee or tea.

For example, at my placement, the person who answered the phone in the office had a detailed knowledge of local mental health services—you could name any area, and she would tell you who was in charge of it and what provision there was. Speaking with her opened my eyes to the different agencies, types of support, and, in particular, who was in charge there (which meant I knew who to email or phone in the future, if need be).

Similarly, the other therapists at your placement will have a wealth of information. Students are like a goldmine, because they're learning all the time, and therefore possess so much new information—and the enthusiasm to share this information. I can remember some wonderful conversations with other therapists (some on different types of courses, and others with more experience), filling the gaps in my knowledge.

Training and CPD (Continual professional development)
Enquire at your placement whether any training or CPD opportunities are provided. Some agencies offer free or subsidised courses. For example, a lot of bereavement charities want you to undertake a course in bereavement, perhaps even before you start work there.

Supervision
Some agencies offer group supervision, which you may be able to claim as part of the course requirements, which will save money on individual supervision, or perhaps even take on more client hours. Always check out these possibilities first with your course tutor.

Staff Committees
Some agencies have a staff committee, which you may be able to join. This can give you valuable experience in how the third sector (i.e. a charity) operates, and you may gain access to service commissioners (i.e. funders). This can be valuable if you think you might wish to start your own charity in the future. You can begin to understand the structure of the sector, how it works, and the hoops you need to jump through to be awarded funding. This would also be invaluable knowledge if you apply for a job at a charitable agency.

Research Projects

The final stage of counselling training typically requires students to undertake a research project. When you are doing this, you can ask your agency whether there are any issues they'd like you to research. This will not only give you a topic, but also look impressive on your CV, showing you are a serious researcher.

Policies and Procedure

If possible, get copies of your agency's policies and procedures. Many courses ask you to provide evidence of your understanding of these things. Being familiar with them will also help you operate professionally in your placement.

I hope that these tips will be useful for you. It is amazing how much you can get out of your placement, if you know what to ask and where to look.

Chapter 7

Working in a
Multidisciplinary Team

Possible Contexts

If you work for an organisation that isn't purely a counselling agency—for example, a school, hospital or hospice—then you are likely to be working as part of a multidisciplinary team. It's important to know how information sharing works in this context.

History

The importance of appropriate information sharing among professionals was highlighted in 2000 by the case of Victoria Climbié, a young girl who was murdered by her aunt and uncle. As the investigation unfolded, it became clear that most of the professionals working with the family knew a little of what was going on, but that nobody had the full picture.

One of the exercises I did as a lecturer was to split my class into four or five groups, give each group a little piece of information, and ask what they could make of it. They found that they couldn't make much sense of this, but that when they were subsequently able to put it all together with the other groups, the meaning and implications became much clearer.

Contracting

It is the contract that lays out for clients the limits of confidentiality. As counsellors, we don't work with secrets—we work with confidential information. At the beginning of the first session, contracting gives clients the autonomy to make an informed choice about whether or not they wish to proceed, given that you may need to break confidentiality (e.g. in the case of harm to self or others, or serious crime such as terrorism, money laundering, or drug trafficking).

Information Sharing

In a multidisciplinary environment, the contract will reflect with whom it may be necessary to share information. For example, if you're working in a school, your contract may state that you may have to share information with a parent or with child protection. The extent of information sharing will be guided by your organisation and its policies.

Guiding Principles

The Caldicott principles are used to guide information sharing between professionals. The Caldicott report (so named because the committee that produced it was led by Dame Fiona Caldicott) followed a review commissioned in 1997 by England's Chief Medical Officer following increasing concerns about the use and storage of patient information in the NHS. The Caldicott report can be very useful to us as therapists, as a guide to how, why, and when we can and should share information. There were originally six Caldicott principles, with a seventh added in 2012. The seven Caldicott principles are as follows:[17]

1. **Justify the purpose of using personal confidential information.** If we need to share confidential information, we must justify the purpose of this. This may be referred to as "defensible decision making"—meaning that if we are questioned about why we broke confidentiality, we can defend ourselves and explain our reasons.

2.   **Don't use personal confidential information unless it's absolutely necessary.** In other words, we don't share information unless we have to. Again, this links strongly to the concept of defensible decision making.

3.   **Use the minimum necessary personal confidential information.** For example, suppose a client says to you that they're thinking of taking their life — they have a specific plan, and are in possession of the necessary equipment to follow through with this. In this case, you would break confidentiality only about the details of the plan (e.g. method and timing), and not, for example, about their relationships or past. In other words, you would share only the information that was critical to the reason you were breaking confidentiality.

4.   **Access to personal confidential information should be on a strict need-to-know basis.** An example here would be that my home office contains a locked filing cabinet, plus a password-protected computer. I am the only person who can access information in these places. In other words, it is not appropriate to have people opening filing cabinets and browsing through other people's personal data.

5.   **Everyone with access to personal confidential information should be aware of their responsibilities.** That is, if I have information — clients' names, addresses and telephone numbers — I have to be aware of what my responsibilities are under the GDPR.

6. **Understand and comply with the law.** Every use of personal data must be lawful, and someone in each organisation must be responsible for making sure that it complies with the legal requirements. In my case as a private-practice counsellor, I'm the responsible person. For every large organisation, there is a staff member who serves as the Caldicott guardian.

7. **The duty to share information can be as important as the duty to protect confidentiality.** For example, suppose a client arrives for counselling under the influence of drugs or alcohol, and seems (to you) incapable of driving home safely. To prevent the person from causing an accident (and therefore bringing harm to themselves and others), it would be a principled and defensible decision to inform the police.

Working in a multi-disciplinary team requires that everyone understands their role and the limits of confidentiality. A client needs to be aware of how, and in what situations information needs to be shared. All of this should be made clear in the contract before any therapeutic work commences.

Chapter 8

Assessing Clients

History of Assessment

Assessment has always been part of a person-centred therapy, although it wasn't always known as "assessment", and little was written about it in the early days. However, it's clear that assessment did take place. For example, Gloria Szymanski, who featured in Everett Sholstrom's film, *Three Approaches to Psychotherapy* (1965), was handpicked for this, already having had experience with therapy.

Purpose of Assessment

So why is assessment important for contemporary therapists? In summary, it supports us to provide the best possible service to clients, and so also to protect our own and the profession's reputation. For example, in an agency setting, assessment is typically carried out by a qualified and experienced practitioner. They see clients initially, screen them, and then allocate them to therapists based on the therapist's level of skill, knowledge, and experience. This enables the client to receive the most appropriate care, and the therapist to work within their ability. The client deserves to have a therapist who is competent in working with the presenting issues; moreover, this is important in meeting the requirements of the *Ethical Framework for the Counselling Professions*, published by the British Association for Counselling & Psychotherapy.

Areas for Assessment

Assessment is typically used to look at a number of key areas:

- **client's needs** – determining what the client wants to change, and what issues they think they would like to bring to therapy

- **client's expectations** – explaining what counselling is, how it works, and what it is realistic to achieve – helping to avoid "magic wand syndrome", where clients expect to be cured in a few sessions

- **health and safety** – ensuring that the client is not in crisis or trauma, and is able to make psychological contact (e.g. is not under the influence of substances, or experiencing psychosis or hallucinations)

- **diversity** – ascertaining, for example, whether the client needs an interpreter, wheelchair access, or a hearing loop (ensuring that we meet the requirements of relevant legislation: in the UK, the Equality Act 2010), or wants to see a specific gender of therapist

- **type of counselling** – identifying what modality and specialty would be most beneficial for the client's issues and preferences, e.g. allocating someone with arachnophobia—a fear of spiders—to a cognitive behavioural therapist rather than a person-centred counsellor; and someone with a kinaesthetic (physical/tactile) learning style to a therapist who facilitates clients to use clay, figures, or objects to explain how they are in the world).

Signposting to Other Agencies

As a result of assessment, it's possible that the assessing counsellor may choose to signpost the client to other sources of support, either instead of or before counselling. For example:

- if someone has just been bereaved of their partner, and then discovered that the person who died had borrowed the entire equity of the house and so they are about to be made homeless, they may first need financial advice

- if a client who wants counselling also needs help withdrawing from alcohol or drugs, it may be better to first go to an agency that supports that, thus helping them to enter counselling in a position to make full psychological contact

- if the person is experiencing psychosis, they may be better helped by acute mental health services.

Getting the Timing Right

My good friend, Bob Cooke, from the Manchester Institute for Psychotherapy, says: "Therapy is a process, not an event." In other words, change is made not just in one session, but through a series of them. So if a client has a very chaotic lifestyle—perhaps due to issues around childcare, debts, crisis, or moving around—and so is unable to commit to regular appointments, you must consider whether it's ethical to start opening someone up. If they begin to open up, then are unable to return for more sessions, you may have done more harm than good.

The other thing I'm always curious about is why people have sought therapy. It can be useful for clients to understand this. For example, people who have been abused often present for therapy when their children reach the age at which they experienced the abuse. They somehow see themselves in their children, and it can be very useful for them to understand that this is happening, because the client can then link the two things.

Transference and Countertransference
Sometimes, we get really strong feelings about a client, and that can come from our own history. Maybe the work with a client, or the way they speak, reminds you of someone you know or knew. Many years ago, I met with a supervisee who felt terrified of her client, even though he had given her no reason for this. He didn't look or sound like anyone from the client's past. Eventually, I asked, "What does he smell like?" And the supervisee sat up and said, "That's it! He smells like the person who abused me."

In a case like this—where transference is taking place—it's important to take a highly principled view on whether you, as the assessing therapist, could work with this client, because there may be personal work for you to do first. Smell, in particular, can be very tricky, because it's really embedded into the brain. This sense is located in the olfactory bulb and the limbic system of the brain, and so can trigger people. In a case like this, onward referral—if you are working in private practice and cannot therefore allocate the client to a colleague in the agency—may well be the most ethical approach.

Use of Assessment Notes
So should the counsellor who is subsequently allocated to the client read the assessment notes or not? I never used to read them,

as I felt it was an important principle in person-centred therapy to hear the client's voice directly, rather than through any filter. But over the years, I've realised that sometimes—especially with very complex presentations around abuse, neglect, or trauma—clients might not want to talk about triggering events again. Certainly there's some evidence that retelling the story of traumatic events can re-traumatise the client. So, sometimes, it's useful simply to say, "You know, I've read the referral." Also, you could get a great deal of detail in the referral, giving you a good overview for the client before you start working with them.

Risk

Client referrals sometimes contain information on risk, either to the client or to others. It is crucially important that anyone referring a client makes the recipient aware of risk issues. Referral highlights areas of risk that make you self-aware of any potential triggers, which may escalate any possible harm. If in doubt, speak to the referrer before offering a client an appointment.

Student Counsellors and Assessment

Should students assess clients? Although a qualified counsellor will have done the initial assessment at the agency, my view is that the student should do a soft assessment when they first see the client, because things can change. There's a good possibility that the client you are seeing has been on the waiting list for a while. Even within a month, a lot can change. It's simply a good habit to re-assess clients at the first counselling session, making your practice life a lot easier and making you a more ethical practitioner.

Chapter 9

Boundaries in Counselling

Ethical Context

The BACP *Ethical Framework for the Counselling Professions* makes reference to core principles. Directing attention to important ethical responsibilities, these principles are:[18]

- **being trustworthy** – honouring the trust placed in the practitioner
- **autonomy** – respect for the client's right to be self-governing
- **beneficence** – a commitment to promoting the client's well-being
- **non-maleficence** – a commitment to avoiding harm to the client
- **justice** – the fair and impartial treatment of all clients, and the provision of adequate services
- **self-respect** – fostering the practitioner's self-knowledge, integrity, and self-care.

Major Boundaries

The *Ethical Framework* is useful in talking about the key boundaries we must not cross. For example, it says that we will not have sexual relationships with—or behave sexually towards—our clients, supervisees or trainees. Also, we will avoid having sexual relationships with people who are close to our clients in order to avoid undermining our clients' trust in us.

It also refers to dual relationships, meaning that it's important to avoid counselling your next-door neighbour or someone from your workplace. When I worked as a placement counsellor many years ago, there were quite a few people on the waiting list who I knew personally. And I would write a little note saying, "Do not refer to Rory", because I knew them, so it would have been a dual relationship.

Regular Boundary Issues

The boundary issues discussed above are major ones—and therefore more obvious. However, there are also many other boundary issues that crop up much more regularly in counselling, but that may be more subtle and so much harder to spot. How do we use our own moral compass and insights gained from supervision to identify these and to walk an ethical path? The following sections explore a few such issues.

Rescuing – This is a classic boundary issue. For example, a therapist might tell a client, "Everything will be all right." In doing this, they are trying to make things okay—showing sympathy rather than empathy.

Time Management – Another area that gets overlooked is time management. Letting sessions run over, turning up late, or rescheduling sessions at a time that's inconvenient for the therapist are all boundary issues—and they neglect your self-care. If you find yourself doing this, it may be worth asking yourself why. Of course, there may be times when there's a genuine emergency and the practitioner has to take a view. But if it's happening regularly, then that becomes a boundary issue.

Transference – One of the hidden areas of boundaries (which sometimes isn't discussed in training) is transference. Being therapists, we try to be in an adult place in our interventions, whether supervising, teaching or counselling. It's important that we mirror good practice and show an adult perspective of ourselves, which in turn helps us be more efficient and more engaged in the work.

But what happens if we get a client who reminds us of someone from our past? Say, for instance, you get somebody who reminds you of an authority figure from your past, and you subconsciously slip into a child ego state where you're wanting to please, or where you feel frightened? That could be a boundary issue, because the emotional state of the therapist informs the type of interventions—e.g. the reflections and paraphrases—and the general way they behave with the client.

Thus, it's extremely important that we have a sense of ourselves as adults—and if (for whatever reason) we find ourselves with child-like or parental feelings, we seek the input of our supervisor, to try and find out what that's about. It's also important to develop your "self/internal-supervisor"—in other words, that part of you that sits on your shoulder rather like Jiminy Cricket (the character that served as Pinocchio's moral compass). Jiminy Cricket would whisper in Pinocchio's ear, "Hey, are you sure you're doing the right thing? You know, this is what could happen."

Ever-Shifting Nature of Boundaries – Boundaries are not always clear-cut, nor are they necessarily constant and fixed. It's important to always be looking out for boundary issues—and to be willing to reflect and to seek help from your supervisor (and personal counsellor, if appropriate) to ensure that you are getting it as right as possible in this important area of ethical practice.

Chapter 10

Contracting in Counselling

Our clients deserve the best possible service. One of the ways we can be sure this is happening is to make a contract at the beginning of therapy so the client knows exactly what they are getting, and they can make an informed choice.

Nature of a Counselling Contract

A counselling contract is an overview of the service a counsellor offers a client. It should include various elements, which are outlined in the following sections.

Modality of Therapy
Few clients will be familiar with different modalities of therapy, and what they mean in practice. For example, I usually explain person-centred therapy by saying, "I'll give you the space to help you discuss what's going on for you, to feel that you've been heard, and to try and make sense of where you're at."

Number of Sessions Offered
If you are working in an agency, there may be a maximum of six sessions offered to each client. You would mention whether this could be extended (often at the managerial supervisor's discretion), if the client wants this.

Supervision Arrangements
It's important to tell your client the people with whom you will discuss client work—i.e. your arrangements for individual, group

and/or peer supervision—explaining that the client's identity isn't disclosed, and that it's more about discussing presenting issues in order to ensure we offer the best possible service.

Access to Notes

If you work for an agency, the law says that all the work you do for them in that time belongs to them. This would include the writing of notes. The agency might allow you to store these notes externally, but it's usual to require them to be stored in a locked filing cabinet on the premises. You might want to ask your managerial supervisor who has access to this.

The other people who can access your notes are:
- the client, under the Data Protection Act 2018 (the UK's implementation of the General *Data Protection Regulation*)
- a judge, with a court order (not simply the police, who can request a client's notes but—if the client refuses to consent to disclosure—must get a court order)
- a coroner (in the case of a client dying).

Limits of Confidentiality

There are three legal areas in which we are not obliged to maintain confidentiality—drug trafficking, money laundering, and acts of terrorism. In these three situations, I would not be able to tell the client that I have disclosed the apparent crime. The legal complications of perverting the course of justice mean that if you are seen to have tipped someone off, you could get yourself into a lot of trouble.

As well as the limits of legal confidentiality, I also talk about the limits of agency confidentiality. Currently, there is no law in the

UK that compels a therapist to disclose actual or suspected child abuse.* It is likely that your agency will have its own policy on this, as well as on harm to self and others.

Complaints Procedure

Another thing that should be in a contract is how to access the complaints procedure, if something goes wrong. As an independent practitioner, I always make it clear to my clients that I am a member of the BACP. That would be the route to complain that a client would follow if need be. If you work for an agency, the typical route would be to make a complaint to the agency. If it couldn't be resolved within the agency, then the complaint would go to the BACP. But there is no barrier to a client going straight to the BACP and not going through the agency.

Terms and Conditions of Payment

This applies if you are in private practice, or if your agency charges a certain fee per session. It's important that the client knows when they must pay, what methods they can use, and where they stand in terms of obligation to pay the fee if they need to cancel a session.

Reasons for Counselling Contracts

Moving on from the contents of a typical counselling contract, why is it important to have a contract? The contract gives clients the information they need to make an informed choice and to have some power in the counselling relationship. As a counsellor, you're always trying to balance the power dynamic between yourself and your clients, but sometimes it's very difficult. One of the things that you'll never fully balance out is the fact that they are coming to you because they've got a problem they want to resolve. This always tips the balance in the counsellor's favour. But one way we can make sure that it doesn't tip any further is by having a clear contract. This gives people a sense of power in that they know what they're getting.

Giving Clients a Copy of the Contract

Should the client get a copy of the contract? I believe that they definitely should—and this links strongly to the values of autonomy and justice, both of which are mentioned in the *Ethical Framework for the Counselling Professions*, published by the BACP.

This allows the client to have a good look at the contract in private. I ask my clients to sign the contract in the first session, but then at the second session, I gently touch on this, saying, "I wonder if you've looked through the contract. Is it okay for you?" This is a good way of double-checking that they're comfortable with it, and helping them understand their importance in the counselling relationship, and that they have a choice.

Written versus Verbal Contracts

It's good practice to have a written contract so that both parties are clear and can make reference to it. If a complaint is made to an ethical body, they'd almost certainly asked for a copy of the contract. If you don't have a copy, you're relying on remembering and evidencing spoken words, which can be very difficult. If both you and your client have a copy of the contract, there is proper clarity.

Other Forms of Contracts

Some counsellors also have a "therapy contract". This is a separate (usually verbal) contract, where the client outlines what they wish to work toward and change.

Therapy contracts are mostly used in TA, because they form part of this model of therapy. Eric Berne, the founder of TA, believed that if you sit a client down and ask them what they want to change, then they will work toward it. When the change has been achieved, then the contract is finished. You could then ask the client, "Is there anything else you would like to change?" This may lead to a fresh contract.

In person-centred therapy, the therapy contract is not as formal and as cut-and-dried as this. However, I gently ask the client what it is that they're looking to change through therapy. This forms the basis of a "soft" therapeutic contract, and references a goal to which you can return. For example, later in therapy you might say, "When you first came, you said you wanted to change this. And I've noticed from what you've just said that you've now done this.' This can help the client realise the progress they have made.

At the time of publication, the UK Government has published 'Reporting and acting on child abuse and neglect. Summary of consultation responses and Government action'. This consultation document invites representatives from public services such as educators, social workers and the police—as well as third sector organisations such as the NSPCC or any agency who comes into contact with children—to shape government policy in the area of mandatory reporting of child abuse.

Consultation documents are the first stage of governments enacting legislation which becomes a legal requirement.

To view the consultation document, scan this QR-Code (will use your phone data).

Chapter 11

Law in Counselling
Contracts

Contracting

Contracting is done at the very beginning of therapy, ideally using a written document that is then signed by both client and supervisor. In the UK, there is a television programme titled *Judge Rinder*, on which barrister Robert Rinder oversees civil court cases. He speaks frequently about the importance of written contracts—to protect both the provider and the receiver of services.

Within the contract, it is important to describe the limits of confidentiality. This means that if you ever need to break confidentiality, you have a written record of the client having agreed to these limits (i.e. you have evidence of your defensible decision making). My contracts are signed by both myself and the client. Also, at the next session, I say (out of respect for the client), "*I just want to check whether you are okay with the contract, and that you understand the limits of confidentiality.*"

Limits to Confidentiality

One of the key areas of counselling in which it is important to understand the law, is in the limits to confidentiality. But before examining this, let's look at the meaning of "confidentiality" in the context of counselling. Confidentiality is not secrecy; instead, it involves agreeing with your client the limits of what you can share with others. In the UK, three main laws are relevant to setting and explaining the limits of confidentiality:

- **Terrorism Prevention and Investigation Measures Act 2011**
  There is absolutely no justification for a therapist not to disclose any activity that could be terrorism-related—because terrorism can cause harm to huge numbers of people. If a client disclosed that a terrorist attack was being planned, you would need to break confidentiality.

- **Drug Trafficking Act 1994**
  While selling small amounts of cannabis or other drugs—illegal as it is—would not require an automatic breach of confidentiality, trafficking large amounts (e.g. shipping them in containers or lorries) would. If you are ever unsure about whether you should break confidentiality, it's best to discuss this with your supervisor or professional body.

- **The Money Laundering, Terrorist Financing and Transfer of Funds (Information on the Payer) Regulations 2017**
  Money laundering occurs when someone tries to conceal large amounts of money that they have gained through illegal means; this is commonly done through transfers involving foreign banks or through legitimate businesses. For example, a person who had £100,000 in drug money might open a fish-and-chip shop and then "launder" the money through this business, pretending they've sold £100,000 worth of food so that they can then put the cash in the bank, passing it off as legitimate earnings.

Other Crimes

There is currently no legal obligation for therapists to disclose "low-level" crimes. Sometimes therapists might feel they need to break confidentiality, because clients may harm themselves or others. For example, I had a colleague whose client presented under the influence of alcohol; they had driven to the appointment, and were planning to drive home again. My colleague offered to call a cab for the client, who refused this. My colleague therefore made the decision to call the police, and the person was arrested for drinking and driving.

Data Protection Act 2018

Under this law, which is the UK's implementation of the GDPR, clients have the right to access the counselling notes that you write about them.

Other than the clients themselves, the only people who are entitled to access your notes are judges with a court order, or coroners (where a client has died). Thus, if your client was going through a divorce and their partner phoned you up and asked for your notes, you would not provide them.

I have had cases where the police have contacted me and asked me for my notes. I have replied politely, "If the client wants the notes, I will give the notes to them and they can pass them on." If the client does not wish to do this, then I have had to say respectfully, "I'm afraid you will have to get a court order in that case." In cases such as these they have understood and accepted this, with the caveat that they may have to get a court order.

Specific Client Groups

There are exceptions to confidentiality that come with working with certain client groups. For example, if you're working in a drug rehabilitation service with people who are in recovery or in active addiction, your clients may well be taking prescribed medication to manage the drugs cravings. This is specifically prevalent if somebody is using heroin or an analgesic (painkiller), where they may be given a substitute to manage their withdrawal. The difficulty is that if they also take street drugs, they could die (a phenomenon sometimes referred to as "going over"), for example through a heart attack. A drug rehabilitation services counselling contract may very state the use of street drugs would have to be disclosed.

Working with Children

Surprisingly, there is (at the time of writing) no legal obligation for a counsellor in private practice to break confidentiality if a child discloses they are being abused. However, most child therapy takes place under the umbrella of an organisation (e.g. a school or a young people's charity), within which its own policies would have mandatory reporting of child abuse.* *See the appendices in the chapter Contracting.*

Policies and Procedures

While the BACP's *Ethical Framework for the Counselling Professions* is the baseline for confidentiality, the agency's policies and procedures may have additional elements with regard to confidentiality. The key point here is that you must ensure that the client understands the limits of confidentiality—that is why it is so important to have a written and signed contract.

Resources

As useful reading on this topic, I would recommend *Counselling, Psychotherapy and the Law*, written by Peter Jenkins.[19]

If you are struggling with issues of confidentiality, speak with your supervisor and/or your professional body. If you're in training, you could also ask your tutors. Above all, remember that the contract is your safety net: it protects you as much as the client.

Chapter 12

Reviewing Client Progress

Pros and Cons

Reviewing clients' progress in therapy is a contentious area, with some person-centred therapists and supervisors arguing that this comes from the counsellor's—not the client's—frame of reference. They prefer to let the clients just be, and to explore what's going on for them.

The counter position is that the review process may help clients to assess what's changed for them, in order to validate progress and to focus on what other issues may need to be addressed in their remaining sessions. We live in a world where numerous counselling services—especially those providing free therapy—limit counselling (typically offering a maximum six to twelve sessions). Unlike unlimited therapy, it may be useful to agree at the very beginning what the client wants to change. The client may need support in doing this, especially if they are feeling existentially out of sorts and not connected. For example, you might decide together to work on anxiety, relationships, or patterns of behaviour. Do be careful, however, when mentioning how many sessions the client has remaining; this may make them feel pressurised to "work harder".

In other cases, review can occur naturally. For example, a client might spontaneously refer to a change in self that they've noticed.

Other Modalities

In classic TA, Eric Berne wrote a lot about contracts. He believed that you should develop a therapeutic contract with the client, identifying what they want to change. You should then work through the arc of therapy, focusing on the desired change. At the end, the therapeutic contract is fulfilled; the client could then choose to look at another issue or to go away and celebrate their change of script (to use a TA term).

In CBT, many therapists use measures to gauge how sensitive people are to particular situations or environments.

Assessment Tools

In many healthcare settings, and certainly in the UK's National Health Service, assessment questionnaires are completed at the start and end of therapy (and maybe in the middle too) to ascertain how much the client has improved through therapy. Common tools here include GAD-7, PHQ-9 and CORE-10.

It can be useful for students to use reviews in order to gain a sense of therapeutic change and to support work with their supervisors.

Good Practice in Reviewing

During contracting, it's important to explain that reviews are part of the way you practise, so these don't come as a surprise to clients. Assuming that you have a choice whether to undertake reviews with clients, you can ask the client how they feel about this. It can be helpful to point out that the reviews are not a judgement on their performance, but rather an exploration of where the client is in the therapy process. You could also explain that reviews offer an opportunity for you to ask the client if there is anything more they need. This can really strengthen the therapeutic alliance.

I would also suggest giving at least one session's notice before the review. The client doesn't want to come in and then have a review sprung upon them. Above all, be gentle and respectful. Consider whether you need to review, because all clients are different.

Pitfalls in Reviewing

First, don't be dogmatic. If, on the day of the review, a client wants to focus on another topic, then work with what they want to bring. Don't push your original agenda. You need to work with the immediacy of what the client is bringing.

Second, don't give the impression that if a client feels they have no progress to reflect on, they have failed. In fact, the client's belief that nothing has changed reveals a channel for more exploration of where the client is, opening a whole new therapeutic vista. Sometimes, you may be able to point out progress that you've observed in the client.

Similarly, remember that progress is a relative thing. What may appear as a small movement to you may be massive for the client. Sometimes, behaviour change is a very gradual process, with trial-and-error and fear/anxiety attached to it. So, even a small amount of progress is positive.

In summary, remember that therapy is a process, not an event.

Chapter 13

Stages in Counselling

Key Stages

There are three key stages in the counselling relationship: the beginning, middle and end. Each comprises a specific type of work that needs to be done for the arc of therapy to take effect. This chapter examines these stages in turn.

Beginning Stage
The initial stage is contracting. This is important because it gives the clients an opportunity to learn what the counsellor has to offer, times and durations of the appointments, and limits to confidentiality. Other aspects of contracting include explaining how the client can make a complaint or access their notes, and exploring what issues the client wants to bring. Thus, contracting addresses the important ethical consideration which means the client has autonomy over whether they wish to engage in counselling.

Contracting can also help to address (to some extent) the power imbalance within the counselling relationship. If you think about it, there's a lot of power stacked up on the side of the counsellor, especially when these are provided free of charge. For example, the client tends to go to the counsellor's premises at the time that the counsellor sets; the session lasts a set time; and there are a set number of sessions on offer.

Finally, contracting builds trust. Starting the therapeutic relationship on this professional basis means that the client can feel secure that they're working with a practitioner who takes their work seriously. And if something goes wrong, they can go back to the contract to help redress this.

Middle Stage
In the middle stages of counselling, the therapeutic relationship continues to develop and the therapeutic work is carried out. During this time, the client discusses and explores the difficulties they're facing and, with support of the counsellor, may either find acceptance or explore making changes. For some clients (e.g. those who have been ignored or abused), simply being heard and believed can be highly therapeutic.

Ending Stage
If you are working with a fixed number of sessions (e.g. as is common in the charitable sector), you will have discussed this with the client during contracting. It is good practice to remind them now and then—and certainly at the halfway point in therapy—where they are in the course of sessions. This helps to prepare them for the ending, so that it doesn't come as a frightening surprise.

It could become clear to both parties before the maximum number of sessions that the client is ready to disengage from the relationship. For example, the client may feel they have nothing left that they need or want to speak about.

Preparation for endings can include a discussion about the work done, and an acknowledgement of the journey taken. This provides an opportunity for the counsellor to highlight the changes that the client has made, and how far they have come. Particularly when the number of sessions is limited, it can also be an opportunity to map support going forward, whether through the same agency (e.g.

other in-house services, such as groups and activities) or through another organisation. It might be that the client makes their own appointment or that you make a referral on their behalf.

It's really important to achieve as good an ending as possible. Badly managed endings form the basis of many complaints to the BACP. So always prepare and plan for the ending with your clients.

Chapter 14
The Skill of Attending

Links to Unconditional Positive Regard (UPR)

As one of the most underrated skills, attending links directly to the core condition of UPR. The skill of attending is about putting the client in the centre of your universe for the time that you're working with them. For a client who's not being cared for or loved, or who feels rejected, having someone who is really hearing them may be a particularly unusual and powerful experience. There's a real difference between listening and hearing. Listening is just paying attention, but hearing links into the other skills of reflecting emotions, paraphrasing, and summarising.

Timeline for Attending

Attending starts from the very first moment you meet the client. That could be on the phone when you make the first appointment, or when you meet them in person and welcome them into your therapy room. Attending goes on through the arc of therapy—until they finish and move out into the world and don't see you again.

Body Language

The skill of attending must be seen and accepted by the client in order to be effective.

We can help achieve this in various ways, many of which relate to our body language.

For example, you can use eye contact to show that you are attending to a client. Try to be as natural as possible when doing this, and avoid looking as if you're staring at them. Bear in mind that while eye contact is one of the ways that westerners show they are listening, it can be interpreted differently by other cultures. For example, in Asian countries, eye contact can be seen as disrespectful. And in some other cultures, it can be seen as a sign of aggression. So it's important to be culturally sensitive when using eye contact.

The way we sit can also give important clues about how much we are listening. Being relaxed and comfortable helps us to focus on the client and not ourselves. In addition, leaning forward can help to indicate how intently you're listening to the client. In my practice, if a client is talking about very difficult material, I find myself moving closer to them (always checking that the space between us still feels comfortable and respectful to them). For me, it's a sign to say, "No, I'm not shying away from this. I really want to hear this and help you." It can be powerful to see someone leaning in and showing that they're paying attention. Conversely, sitting with arms crossed can be seen as a barrier to attending, as can waving your arms about. While some people like to gesticulate when talking, this can put off some clients.

Environmental Factors
Another action that shows good attending skills is making sure that access to the room and the room itself are appropriate for counselling. Overall, we must do what we can to make sure that the room is comfortable and safe. More specifically, under the Equality Act 2010 in the UK, we have to make reasonable adjustments. That might be a hearing loop for people who have hearing difficulties, or it may be access for people who are wheelchair users.

It's possible that some clients may have specific wishes; where possible, we should try to accommodate these. For example, I've read of a therapist covering up a mirror in their practice room for a client who was struggling with their self-image. Other clients may dislike certain sounds in the room (e.g. a ticking clock). Recently, a complaint that was upheld by the BACP included the fact that a client had asked for certain things not to be in the room but the therapist hadn't removed them: that was a lack of attending. In short, it's important to accommodate client wishes if you can reasonably do so.

Endings

Attending also involves paying attention to endings. Endings are one of the most important parts of the therapeutic arc (another being openings). In order to maximise the chance of having a good ending, try to ensure that the ending is planned. It would be completely disrespectful—and potentially even frightening—to spring an ending on a client.

If you're working to a number of fixed sessions—as many student therapists (typically in charitable agencies) will be—it's useful to speak with the clients about endings in advance, and to be thoughtful about signposting other support as you approach the end. If a client is coming to the end of therapy and feels they need more support, help them map their support network; you might perhaps choose to make an appropriate referral.

In summary, remember—as Greek philosopher Epictetus (50AD-135AD) observed—there's a reason we have two ears and one mouth: so we can listen twice as much as we speak. This is a really good balance of our responding and listening in the therapy room.

Chapter 15

Transference in the
Therapy Room

What Is Transference?

Transference happens when one person inadvertently relates to another as if they were a significant person from their past. When this happens, we don't treat the other person as a new one we've never met before, and approach them openly. Instead, we bring all the emotions and experience of that person from the past and apply it undeservedly to the person in front of us. In other words, we allow the past to influence the present. Because of its often-subconscious nature, transference can be very tricky to spot.

Examples of Transference and Counter-Transference

When I was working as a college lecturer, one of my students was very concerned about a client she was working with. When she was with him, she felt petrified, yet the man was not doing anything real that explained her fear. She had reflected on this herself, and discussed it with her supervisor: we all agreed that there must be some transference going on. In other words, the client must remind her of someone from her past.

We investigated all kinds of possible avenues, wondering whether the reminder might relate to physical appearance, words, hand gestures, style of dress etc. Nothing fit until I hit upon another question: how did the client smell? My learner bolted upright and said, "*That's it! He reminds me of an abusive ex-partner, he smells like him.*" So here we can see Transference, but what about Counter-Transference? In this case, my student had started to become frightened and unsure of herself. Feelings she would have experienced in the past when interacting with her abusive partner.

By understanding this, the student could begin to see this client as a new and different person—not as the person from her past who had frightened her.

Another example from a similar time involved me as the object of transference. Once, a student came to me after class and asked whether she irritated me. I replied that she certainly did not, and wondered out loud why she might feel that way. Further discussion revealed that I looked and sounded rather like her father, who had told her that she irritated him. Having understood this context, I was then able to help her see that although we shared certain physical characteristics, her father and I were not the same. This helped her to relate to me in a healthier manner going forward.

A few weeks later I was discussing my student in supervision. On close examination, it became clear that some of her behaviours had pushed a few buttons in me, one of them marked 'irritation'.

She was subconsciously seeing me as her father and occasionally acted in a childlike way in class, demanding more of my attention. Given our conversation, I realised this was 'countertransference', her subconscious way of relating to me as she would her father.

It's not surprising that after our discussion she returned to being an engaged adult. Reflecting on this event, it struck me that having an adult conversation and understanding the theory of transference/countertransference, a phenomenon first identified by psychoanalyst Sigmund Freud, aided better communication between us. I for one was clad the conversation happened.

Warning Signs of Transference in Clients

In the context of counselling, the client may experience transference towards you or vice versa.

Signs that you may remind your client of someone from their past include:

- the client becoming angry at you for no clear reason
- the client becoming childlike in how they speak and behave in the therapy room
- the client acting in a way that suggests they may be frightened of you
- the client being worried that you may judge them.

Any of these indicates that your client might not be seeing you as a new person in the here-and-now, but as an old investment in a past relationship.

You could ask the client, *"Do I remind you of anyone from your past?"* If the client responds that you do, then gently remind them that you are not that person. It may go on to reset the therapeutic relationship to one not burdened with the baggage of the past.

Transference in Counsellors

In my years as a clinical supervisor, I've picked up on several signs that indicate there may be a transferential aspect going on in how one of my supervisees relates to a client. I describe these in the following sections, to help you spot when your client may be experiencing transference towards you.

Struggling to Enter the Client's Frame of Reference

If you are finding it hard to focus on the client, and feeling easily distracted, this can be a sign that the client reminds you of someone from your past.

Experiencing Unrelated Feelings

If you are experiencing very high emotions in the therapy room that don't seem to be connected with what the client is sharing, this can be a warning sign that you are experiencing transference. An alternative explanation is that you are picking up the client's incongruence, which may be conveyed by a mismatch between the client's words and body language (in other words, their real emotions are somehow 'leaking out').

Disliking or Over-Liking the Client

Either disliking the client for no apparent reason or liking the client more than might usually be expected is a typical sign of transference.

Thinking about the Client between Sessions

This may happen naturally when you have a client who is experiencing particularly bad difficulties or is engaging in very risky behaviours. But if there is no obvious explanation of this type, then do think about whether you could be subject to transference.

Wanting to Help the Client More than Other Clients

This happened to me—as an experienced practitioner—just a few years ago. My supervisor noticed that I seemed to feel more urgency about helping one particular client than the rest. When we explored it, I realised that the client reminded me of my daughter. Once that had been highlighted, I was able to re-engage with the client and work with her as the person she was.

Looking for an Excuse to Refer a Client On

For a novice therapist, this can be a clear indication of transference. As a clinical supervisor myself, I might ask my supervisee, *"If you and your client were on a train together, there was no one else in the carriage, and it was a two-hour journey with no stops, would you choose to sit next to them?"* The response to this question gives me a good indication of the quality of the therapeutic relationship.

If the supervisee wants to avoid the imaginary person on the train at all costs, I may inquire why this is and ask, *"What feelings does the client evoke in you?"* It's incredible how transference becomes apparent with such a simple question.

Chapter 16

Using Timelines in Counselling

Importance of the Past

Søren Kierkegaard, a Danish philosopher who influenced the thinking of Carl Rogers, stated, "Life can only be understood backwards; but it must be lived forwards."[20] This observation tells us a universal truth about the human condition: that sometimes our here-and-now perceptions are forged by experiences in our past.

Past experiences may leave us with strong emotions, which we carry through into our lives long after the events that generated these feelings have ended. It may be that when these feelings overcome us or are particularly persistent, they fill our waking days and dreaming nights—and we decide to present for therapy.

Over the years, I've seen many clients who have come to therapy unsure about why they feel anxious or depressed. It's almost like these feelings have been with them forever. This is where using a timeline can be useful.

How to Use a Timeline in Counselling

Take a piece of paper—ideally quite a large one (flipchart paper is perfect)—and position it in landscape format. Draw a horizontal line about halfway up, and add a plus sign above the line and a minus sign below it.

Then, ask the client to fill in the timeline with any event they can remember and the age they experienced it. It's important to get them to do this in chronological order, starting from when they were young and ending where they are now. Get the client to grade each event from 1 (low) to 10 (high).

Meaning of the Timeline to the Client
What this exercise may provide is an overview of events—e.g. losses, house moves and hospital stays—together with the intensity of the feelings generated by them. It will highlight the ages at which they experienced these events.

Sometimes, clients express surprise and shock about the number and timing of events. Crucially, the timeline can give an indication of when the client started to feel emotionally (and even physically) unwell. It's also useful for helping the client become aware of themes that connect and cut across different life events and times.

The client may wish to explore one specific event on the timeline in preference to others. They could also add their here-and-now narrative to the timeline (e.g. a client who felt powerless as a child, but who now has other choices).

Working as a Counsellor with a Client's Timeline
As a counsellor, it's important to:

- recognise the achievements, personal growth, life lessons and wisdom generated by the events shown on the timeline
- look at how the client uses negative events to put changes in place
- be aware of how the past informs the future
- understand how the client's past experiences have prepared them to face future challenges

- remember that it's not the event, but rather how the client perceives and feels about the event that influences their coping style.

Proceeding with Caution
Before undertaking a timeline exercise, consider that this work may bring up strong emotions for the client, and make it clear to them that they are free to stop at any time. Make sure that you leave enough time to ground the client before you come to the end of the session.

In line with Kierkegaard's saying, looking back in order to be able to move forward may be where the real counselling work begins.

Chapter 17

Taking Risks in Counselling

Congruence or Judgement?

Perhaps one of the most contentious moments in all of my counselling training happened during the second year of my diploma. Our tutor read a passage from a counselling book in which the author related an interaction with a client who had told him he was consuming four bottles of wine a night. The author replied, *"That's a lot."*

What followed was nothing short of an uproar. Some of the class exploded in indignation that a therapist could be so judgemental and directive. Others in the group countered that speaking the truth was fundamentally congruent, and drinking four bottles of wine a night is quite simply not good for your health. As we all calmed down, the tutor asked us to work in groups and explore what risks we were willing to take in therapy, and why.

An Example from the World of TA

Eight years later, I attended an introductory course in TA, which was taught by an Australian therapist. She spoke about her experiences with a client who had become quite childlike in the therapy room in order to gain her attention as a form of game-playing. She reflected that one day, having become really fed up with this behaviour, she said to him, *"I think that's enough."* She reasoned that her intervention invited him to return to the adult he was, and not get stuck in a parent-child interaction. It struck me that she took a big risk in confronting the client in such a direct way, and wondered how I might deal with the same situation.

Alcohol and Substance Misuse

A few days later, I was sharing this story with someone who had been in recovery from alcohol and substance misuse for a long time. He recalled a time when, in the throes of addiction, he attended a counselling session after having used, and decided halfway through this that he'd had enough, saying to the counsellor, *"I'm off now to pick up my kids from school."* The counsellor replied, *"I wouldn't let you look after my kids in the state you're in."* When I asked how he felt about this, he responded, *"It was the biggest wake-up call I ever had."* At the time when we spoke, he had been clean (his words) for four years.

Pros and Cons of Taking Risks

Going back to the exercise in my diploma class, one of the things I clearly remember was the range of ways in which my peers viewed risk. Some thought that taking risks was something necessary to help the client's own process. Others felt that it was too directive and judgemental, and could damage the therapeutic relationship, meaning that the client might never return. I suspect that this lesson, above all, really informed our future practice.

Limiting the Risk

Over the years, I've reflected on this lesson a lot, especially my tutor's observation that if you take a risk, you're basically taking a chance that something may go wrong (i.e. the client may never return). You can limit the risk by:

- being thoughtful in how you engage with clients
- not taking risks in the early stages of therapy, instead allowing the relationship to form and to develop trust

- acknowledging to the client that some reflections may be hard for them to hear
- staying in "adult" mode
- refusing to join in with transference, counter-transference or projective identification
- using supervision to explore what risk you want to take, or to reflect on the outcome of risks you've taken
- asking yourself, before engaging with the client, "Who am I taking risks for—the client or myself?"
- reflecting on people in your life who have taken a risk and fed back to you things that may have been hard to hear, identifying how this impacted on your personal development and emotional growth.

Effective therapy may not always feel comfortable for the client—or indeed for the therapist.

Which is why we say to clients at contracting, *"Things may get worse before they get better."*

Chapter 18

Making Referrals

Ethical Practice

The BACP *Ethical Framework for the Counselling Professions* refers to the importance of working within our competence. This means that we must consider whether our level of training and our clinical experience are good matches for the client's presenting issues.

We are also required to reflect on any barriers that may hinder or disrupt the therapeutic relationship, and to be confident that the client is getting the service they are asking for and addressing the issues they want to explore.

Clinical Assessment

The time when we make these decisions is during clinical assessment; this process is not the same as being judgemental. For example, it would be important to challenge a client who could not make psychological contact because they attended sessions under the influence of alcohol or drugs, or because they were psychotic (e.g. hearing voices or being disconnected from reality).

As well as these situations, where psychological contact with any counsellor may be impossible, clinical assessment may also reveal other reasons why you are not the right counsellor for a particular client, but working with another practitioner (a counsellor or a different professional) could be helpful to them. The following sections are informed by the work of Kavita Singh, who wrote *Counselling Skills for Managers*.[21]

Counsellor's Proficiency

The client's presenting issues may be beyond the counsellor's proficiency. For example, if a client arrived in my practice wanting help with a personality disorder, the principled and ethical course of action for me would be to make a referral, since I've not been trained in this area.

Similarly, counsellors are obliged to refer on anyone who comes to discuss issues around being adopted unless they are registered as an adoption support agency with Ofsted (and therefore are able to offer specialist adoption services).

Incompatible Personalities

While it would be lovely to think that the core conditions can be shown in every client-counsellor pairing, in reality they sometimes can't. Sometimes, people just don't get on and this interferes with the counselling process. This could be due to transference and countertransference (i.e. you remind them of someone from their past or vice versa) or it may simply be that the two of you are not a good fit to work together.

If this does happen, it's important to try to address it in supervision, but if this doesn't improve the situation, onward referral may be the best thing.

Shared Connections

When you realise that the client's issues are connected to someone that you know too, such as a relative or a friend, the ethical response would be to inform the client that you need to make a referral.

Client Hesitancy

Another reason for referring is if the client is hesitant about disclosing their issues. Sometimes, clients are not ready to disclose what's going on for them. They may struggle with expressing their emotions and it may be that something other than therapy is needed.

Relationship Difficulties
It can happen that, after several sessions, the counsellor feels the relationship is not effective or therapeutic. Part of being a therapist is to continually review whether any therapeutic work is being done. If the client is bringing an issue that they're looking at and want either to change or to learn to live with, then therapy is proceeding. But if the sessions feel more like a comfortable chat, or the client asks you to do things that are not connected with therapy (e.g. provide legal advice or fill in a benefit form), then a referral may be useful.

Endings
Sometimes, clients may be hesitant to finish therapy. They may have finished what they came for, but they like the warmth and familiarity of the counselling session. As a therapist, you must take a principled and ethical view whether you're still offering therapy. If not, then it's important to talk to your supervisor and to consider whether you are being ethical and offering the best possible service to your client.

How to Refer
Referrals should be made collaboratively, with the client at the centre of the decision to refer. It's important to explain why you wish to make the referral, to establish a clear referral pathway, to discuss confidentiality, and to talk about the likely timescale of the referral.

Building Your Knowledge of Agencies
It's really useful to use the time in your counselling placement to learn about what agencies are available locally to take referrals. For example, placement providers will naturally have connections with community mental health teams, and alcohol/drug services.

Supervision

It's important to make good use of supervision to explore any referrals. This can be done either at your regular supervision session, or through a phone consultation between sessions, which many supervisors offer.

Note-Taking

Always document in the client notes your decision to refer, and the rationale for this.

Last but not least, remember that making a referral isn't a sign of weakness or incompetence. Instead, it's a clear indication that you are aware of your professional limits and boundaries, and want to offer your client the best possible service.

Chapter 19

Trauma-Informed Practice

Looking Back
Before the 1980s, Post-traumatic stress disorder (PTSD) as a diagnosis did not exist. Instead, psychological difficulties following trauma were seen as a wide-ranging set of disparate presentations—such as alcoholism, self-harm, and anger-management problems.

Making Connections
It was only when clinicians joined the dots between the various difficulties faced by veterans of the Vietnam War that they identified these symptoms as symptomatic of how the brain processes trauma. More specifically, clinicians began to understand that the way the brain processes trauma in humans is fairly universal— whether for a former soldier who has flashbacks to the war when hearing a firework going off, or for a civilian who becomes terrified on smelling the scent used by a childhood abuser.

Recent Developments
In the last 15 years, our knowledge about the brain and how it processes trauma has grown exponentially. However, the models of therapy that are often taught make little or no reference to this.

A relatively new term in the world of counselling and psychotherapy is "trauma-informed practice". This forms part of the wider technique of psychological education. This is where the practitioner, when appropriate, shares information with the client on how the brain processes trauma.

Examples

A client may say that they feel ashamed that they did not fight back or run away when being abused. In this situation, it can be very powerful to explain that traumatic situations trigger parts of the brain to switch into a form of automatic pilot as a survival strategy—the default option generally being to freeze, or feign death.

Similarly, clients who are conflicted because they felt pleasure while being sexually abused and fear that they must somehow have wanted this can be greatly reassured by understanding that the part of the brain that processes sexual pleasure is disconnected from the part that mediates between right and wrong. This can be very powerful in lifting feelings of shame and guilt.

In short, the words "this is not your fault" cannot be underestimated as a therapeutic response. While models of therapy have been proven to help alleviate mental and emotional distress, using a trauma-informed intervention may very well provide a form of "heavy lifting", moving the weight and shame of the client's natural responses to a traumatic event. With this debris cleared, the client can begin the journey of self-healing, unburdened by the shame and conflicts of their brain's natural responses that are programmed to help them survive.

Chapter 20

Working Within Your Competence

Accepting the Limits of Competence

If a client asked me to write a psychiatric report, I could not ethically agree to do this—because I am not a psychiatrist. Similarly, I would not agree to counsel a couple, as I have not been trained in couples therapy. In other words, we should not seek to work in areas that fall outside our own professional boundaries. In these situations, it is our ethical duty to refer on, signposting people to other professionals who are competent in the issues with which they are seeking assistance.

Feelings of Incompetence

When you are a student starting your counselling placement, everything feels new, and it's not unusual to experience feelings of incompetence. These feelings are very natural: most counsellors have similar feelings at this stage of their training.

Remember that you will be well-supported by your placement (through your managerial supervisor), clinical supervisor, and course tutor. Your professional body—e.g. the BACP, BACP, UKCP or NCS—is an additional source of advice, if needed.

Your Placement

All good placements have a robust referral system in place. So when a client comes to the agency, they are assessed by a qualified, experienced therapist, and then allocated to a suitable counsellor, based on the presenting issue, level of risk, and modality of therapy. For instance, a client who is very complex or who is experiencing suicidal ideation would not usually be referred to a brand new placement counsellor. Nor would a person-centred counsellor be allocated a client who wanted to work on their fear of flying (for which CBT may well be a more appropriate modality).

Clinical Supervision

Having a good clinical supervisor is another vital element in ensuring that you work within—and gradually extend—your competence. A good supervisor will be experienced, have a wide range of training, and have worked with many different client presentations.

CPD

You may get the opportunity to do additional training in preparation for your placement, or while you are working there. For example, many of my students (when I taught counselling) did additional bereavement training. Another possible area for such CPD is trauma. These types of courses can be valuable in extending your knowledge, and so improving your confidence.

Limits of Confidentiality

Part of working for an organisation is to operate within its policies and procedures in terms of confidentiality. It's also important to ensure that you understand and adhere to the ethical expectations of your professional body.

Different counselling agencies may have different limits to confidentiality. For example, if you work in a rehabilitation unit for people who are coming off alcohol and drugs, there may be a specific requirement that you break confidentiality if you become aware that a client is using the relevant substance, as doing so could be dangerous for them in combination with other prescribed medication they may be taking to help the process of withdrawal.

Your Own Process

It's important to be aware of your own process. For example, we might be affected by countertransference—where a client reminds you of someone from your past. This can lead you to respond to them in a way that doesn't reflect the fact that they're a new, unrelated person. Supervision can help you to pick up on this situation. You may well become aware of it yourself when you feel an incongruence within you.

Don't Be Afraid To Ask

Ask for support if you feel that you're working outside your competence. It is perfectly acceptable for therapists of any level of experience to do so. Asking for help doesn't mean that you're doing something wrong, or that you're not competent. It simply means that you need to collaborate with an appropriate person (e.g. your supervisor, your tutor, or maybe one of your peers) to help you make sense of where you are.

All good therapists do this regularly and consistently, because they're checking out their perceptions. After all, Carl Rogers himself observed that we need to check our experience in new and primary ways.

Chapter 21

Working With a Third Person in the Room

Examples of Working With a Third Person

There are times when we may find ourselves working with a third person in the room. For example, we may have a client who is not an English speaker, and so—unless you are bilingual—you will need to work with an interpreter. Or you may have a client who is deaf and uses sign language to communicate. Again, an interpreter may well be needed. Some clients may have a support worker when they come to sessions, because they feel nervous. Last, a third person can even be a recording device—in effect, an unseen person whose presence is silent and unemotional.

Not Ideal, But Still Effective

Lorraine Quinn, a UKCP-registered integrative psychotherapist with an academic background in linguistics and textual criticism, has undertaken research into working with a third person in the room. She observes that working in this way might not always be easy or ideal, but that therapists are generally conscious of the need to find ways to make their work effective, ethical, and as culturally appropriate as possible within the available resources.

Choosing an Interpreter

As a counsellor, you should never let a family member be an interpreter for a client. This is because relatives may have an agenda and may misinterpret what the client said. Also, the client may be unwilling or unable to speak freely about their issues in front of them, particularly if the relative is part of the issues. Interpreters should be neutral and fully trained in interpretation (which is an advanced professional skill in its own right).

Triangulated Contract

Be sure to have a triangulated contract in place so that all three parties are fully aware of their responsibilities, particularly in respect of confidentiality, and organisational policies and procedures. Each person should have a copy of the written contract, which will be different from the contract you would use with just two people in the room.

Recording Devices

If the third person has—or even is—a recording device, it is important to gain the client's explicit written consent. If you are recording client sessions as part of your placement, the agency and/or college may have a form specially designed for this purpose. This should consider the counsellor's obligations under the GDPR—including how you will use the recording and who else might listen to it (e.g. your supervisor or college tutor/peers), how you will store the recording and for how long, and the client's rights to request that it is deleted.

Debriefing the Interpreter

Because of the potentially difficult nature of the material brought in counselling, you may wish to debrief the interpreter or at least speak with them on their own after the session—even if simply making five minutes to check that they are okay. If the client material has somehow touched on a difficult area for them, you could help refer them for therapy themselves.

Lost in Translation?

It may be that an interpreter cannot pick up all the nuances of the client's dialogue, such as a slip of the tongue. Although interpreters are very good, and will interpret not only the words themselves but also the emotion behind these, they may not be able to relay everything after the client has spoken. So it's always worth remembering that sometimes there may be some loss in translation.

Cultural Context

There may also be gains. Lorraine Quinn notes that counsellors may increase cultural insight through working with an interpreter. For example, the interpreter might explain the cultural, social, and historical context for what the client says—so adding to the counsellor's knowledge base, which could be useful in future sessions. One example of this might be providing insights into family dynamics in the relevant culture. Thus, interpreters may be able to offer an added dimension to the counsellor's awareness of the client's frame of reference.

Practical Issues

Remember to always face the client and listen to the interpreter. This can be challenging, as we tend naturally to look towards the person we can understand. Being distracted from the client in this way would take our attention away from the client, and draw us out of the client's frame of reference. You must be highly disciplined about this, as it is not always easy.

Finally, do remember that, as humans, we all share a common language—the language of kindness and compassion—which meets our human need to be heard and validated. This universal language is as much seen and felt as it is heard.

Chapter 22

Hard-to-Help Clients

Never Stop Believing

As a therapist, I really believe that everybody has the capacity to change. This may seem like an optimistic point of view, but it has been guided by many years of experience and by the solid belief that people have the capacity to change, given the right circumstances. It can serve as a guiding light when the going gets tough, and when clients seem very resistant to change, or rather self-defeating.

Reasons for Clients Being Hard to Help

Through the years—in my own experience and in talking to other counsellors—I've identified some of the reasons why clients may self-defeat. Understanding these is the key to being able to work through them and come out the other side, with the client willing to make changes to improve their quality of life. In the following paragraphs, I discuss some of the reasons why clients may be hard to help.

Personal History

First, the client's history may make it difficult for them to be helped. For example, if the client has faced protracted criticism in the past, or if there was a history of violence in the family, significant carers may have been emotionally unavailable for long periods of time.

View of Attachment

Similarly, the client may have unresolved issues regarding death and separation, meaning that they have formed a certain view of attachment—in other words, how they trust people and how they perceive that other people will trust them. This can be very difficult initially as a therapist, as the client simply may not trust you. You may—through no fault of your own—somehow remind them of a person in their past who deserted them (i.e. they might experience transference). In this case, you may have to work quite hard to show yourself as someone who's committed to helping them make change, and to exploring what's going on for them.

Conditions of Worth

Sometimes, it can be difficult if a client has been given conditions of worth or introjected values (known in TA as "injunctions")—that is, messages in their childhood that they have carried through into adulthood. This can affect the client's beliefs and behaviours, meaning that they expect you to fail or to reject them.

Unrealistic Expectations

When the client has idealistic expectations, these can relate to their sense of self-worth. Sometimes, if the client is really struggling, they naturally want to be fixed quickly. As therapists, we know that this is often not possible—there's no magic wand in counselling.

If you have a client who has unrealistic expectations, it's important to discuss this in the contract or to re-contract if it becomes obvious later. It helps to explain patiently what might and might not be able to be done. After all, it's all their work—they are the ones who need to make the changes.

For example, if you have a client who says, "I only need three sessions—I'm sure that you can fix me," it's important to discuss this idea, and maybe explore what "fixing" means to the client.

Social Relationships

Sometimes, social relationships can cause difficulties for clients. For instance, if a client has had difficulty staying in close relationships or feels isolated, it may be that communicating with others—and accessing what's really going on for them—is a real challenge.

Impact of Age

Older clients may have experienced many of their friends dying, and perhaps their family being separated geographically. Also, one of the things about getting older is that people may feel that they "disappear". Certainly in western society, we live in a youth-oriented culture. This means that as people get older, they may be seen as less productive or less useful members of society. In contrast, eastern cultures tend to view older people as having wisdom and as increasing in value as they age.

Neurodiversity

If you have a client who has Asperger syndrome, their ways of communicating and of viewing the world may be very different. This may require the therapist to work very creatively. For example, a friend of mine who has worked with a lot of Aspergic clients will suggest sitting back-to-back—or in separate parts of the room— with a client if they feel anxious about facing her. In one case, she made a small notice (about the size of a playing card) that the client could simply raise if they felt overstimulated by therapy, enabling them simply to leave with no explanation required.

It's important to be willing to understand your client and their style, working with them in a way that feels right and comfortable to them.

Counsellor Process

Of course, when we feel that a client is hard to help, this might reflect on our own process more than theirs.

Transference could feature again here, if the client reminds us of someone from our past in some way. It is all too easy, in this situation, to superimpose our thoughts and feelings about that past relationship onto the client. This prevents us from seeing the real person in front of us, who is a unique individual in their own right.

The difficulty with transference is that it's usually subconscious. So, for example, you—as the counsellor—may feel manipulated, criticised or rejected. Or you may have difficulty trusting a client, or feel that they are challenging the boundaries. This calls for exploration in supervision. I usually ask my supervisees, "If you were on a train going between London and Manchester with no stops and the client [as a stranger] was on the train, would you sit next to them?" The response to this can be quite telling. If a supervisee replies that they wouldn't want to sit next to them, I explore why this might be.

Keeping Hold of the Lifebelt

Whatever the barriers to helping clients, holding on to the very optimistic notion that everybody can be helped and that everybody has the capacity to change is, I think, very useful. Sometimes, it's more than just an optimistic frame of mind—it can be a lifebelt when you are struggling in the sea of hard-to-help clients.

Chapter 23

When Clients Do Not Attend

Frustrations When Clients Do Not Attend Therapy

As a student, I remember sitting in the therapy room alone, reading a book or writing my assignments because my client 'did not attend', often referred to as a "DNA". I also recall looking at my counselling log, hoping that I would accrue the requisite client hours to be able to finish the course at the end of the academic year. At times, I paid for supervision when I had only one or two clients to discuss—wondering whether juggling two paid jobs, study, placement, and personal counselling was really good for my mental health and physical well-being.

Attitude is Everything

It was around this time that I began reading *The Road Less Travelled*, by M. Scott Peck. This book starts off with the pithy observation: Life is difficult.[23] This is one of the greatest truths, because once we see this truth, we transcend it. In other words, once we understand and accept that life is difficult, then life is no longer quite as difficult.

Recognising that nobody's life is easy can help us to accept our own hardships and to be more understanding of others' apparent shortcomings. This truth started to shape my thinking about why clients did not attend, and to soften my feelings in relation to this previous frustration.

Common Reasons for DNAs

Like most therapists who have practised continually for a long period of time—in my case, 15 years at the time of writing—I've come to realise that there are many reasons for clients not returning.

Common reasons I've come across in my own clients, or that I've heard cited by other counsellors, supervisors, and managers of counselling agencies include:

- health problems
- having to work overtime to pay the bills
- needing to look after children or other dependent relatives
- not being ready for counselling
- being unable to pay the bus fare to the agency
- feeling fear or shame
- having to move house.

Other Possible Reasons

While we might imagine that all clients would wish to attend a good number of sessions, sometimes one session is enough. Just to have the chance to offload—and to be heard in that—may help someone to cope and to keep going.

Also, don't underestimate the power of transference. You might possibly remind the client of someone from their past, which makes it difficult for them to keep coming to counselling with you. They might not even be fully aware of this, but just know that they don't feel at ease with you, through no fault of your own.

It's worth remembering that sometimes just putting an hour a week aside for counselling is a luxury that some clients cannot afford. Life can often be busy, and full of responsibilities.

Putting a Positive Spin on DNAs

Frustrating as it is, the upside of a DNA is that you gain a whole hour to read a book, make notes for your assignments, or even go for a walk. Make sure you go to your placement prepared for DNAs, as it's much less frustrating if you have work on hand so that you can use this time fruitfully.

In addition, clients who DNA challenge us to consider how we offer Unconditional Positive Regard—an important learning point for us as counsellors. It's important that we can extend UPR to those who DNA—because we simply never know what is going on in other people's lives.

Chapter 24

Getting Work

Before I share my observations on how to gain employment in counselling, first let me introduce you to the story of:

"The Two Travelers and the Farmer"

A traveller came upon an old farmer hoeing in his field beside the road. Eager to rest his feet, the wanderer hailed the countryman, who seemed happy enough to straighten his back and talk for a moment.

"What sort of people live in the next town?" asked the stranger.

"What were the people like where you've come from?" replied the farmer, answering the question with another question.

"They were a bad lot. Troublemakers—and lazy, too. The most selfish people in the world, and not one of them to be trusted. I'm happy to be leaving the scoundrels."

"Is that so?" replied the old farmer. *"Well, I'm afraid that you'll find the same sort in the next town."*

Disappointed, the traveller trudged on his way, and the farmer returned to his work.

Sometime later another stranger coming from the same direction, hailed the farmer, and they stopped to talk. *"What sort of people live in the next town?"* he asked.

"What were the people like where you've come from?" replied the farmer once again.

"They were the best people in the world—hardworking, honest, and friendly. I'm sorry to be leaving them."

"Fear not," said the farmer. *"You'll find the same sort in the next town."*

The moral to the story is that people see what they want to see, believe what they want to believe. Many people talk themselves out of success and fulfilment by believing in a reality which is not correct, or not seeing the full picture.

Want a real-life example of people who talk themselves out of success? A few years ago, I was teaching a group of students on a public services course—they hoped to be firefighters, police officers or border patrol officers.

We got on the topic of employment and, for the next half hour, were treated to an exciting journey into what I will call the *"failure mindset"*. One learner remarked that the qualification was not an automatic passport to a job, which opened a floodgate of observations such as, *"I don't know why I am doing this qualification if there are no jobs,"* or, *"No one will take us on without experience."*

During a pause in the endless tide of doom and gloom, I remarked, *"From my point of view, this is brilliant news."*

The students looked at me more than a little stunned. I went on, *"I will never have to worry about being up against you in a job interview, as you have already talked yourself out of success."*

Before anyone could respond, Tom came into the class (almost an hour late). "*Late for class, Tom?*" I asked in my best teacher voice. "*Yes*", said Tom, "*I have just been for my final interview with the Fire Service.*"

With all the rest of the students' jaws placed firmly on the desk, Tom explained that he had passed final selection and was just awaiting his medical before being offered a post.

Six weeks before qualifying his course, he had done what his classmates had considered impossible, gaining employment in one of the most competitive professions with the most stringent recruitment criteria.

So, what made Tom different?

He filled in the gaps between what his course provided him with, and what he needed in the world of work he had applied for. He figured out that the Fire Service had some pretty strict physical fitness criteria that had to be evidenced before he had a chance of a job offer. So he ran to and from college every day and undertook circuit training in his lunch break.

He networked with other firefighters, getting valuable insight into what he needed to know outside of the qualification he was taking. He had visited the Fire Service website and downloaded all of the job specifications, giving particular attention to making sure his math and English skills were on the right level (he even enrolled in courses to update his grades).

In his spare time, he volunteered for charities to develop his interpersonal skills and broaden his network. This was a shrewd move, as part of the job role would be liaising with the community he served and communicating with colleagues.

Tom got his dream shot at being a firefighter by securing a job in the county's Fire and Rescue Service.

What has the parable of "The Two Travellers and the Farmer", and the tenaciousness of Tom taught us?

Don't talk yourself out of your rightful success.

Humans have a tendency to invest in their own belief systems. I did this for years, regularly trotting out my life script, that being dyslexic somehow linked to a lack of intelligence and success in life.

It was only when a friend of mine confronted the negative mindset that I carried around for a lot of my life, I understood that if I kept making excuses, I would not get anywhere.

Networking is a useful way of making contacts.

In the counselling world (as in any other form of employment), you will find that most jobs are not advertised—they tend to come from conversations which start, "*Do you know anyone?*" The bigger your network, the more chance you will have of being recommended. Think about what transferable skills you have.

Any job is a mixture of skill sets—have a look at the job specifications and see which skills are being requested. If there are any gaps, fill them in (hint—most jobs want competence in using computers and IT). A qualification on its own is not a passport to paid work.

Finally, don't let others' fears get in the way of your dreams!

As Tom showed us, listening to nay-sayers is not the way to get where you need to be. If counselling teaches us anything, it's that we need to consider our condition of worth and introjected values.

Chapter 25

Developing Your Internal
Supervisor

One of the reasons students have a higher supervision ratio than that of qualified colleagues, is because at the start of their careers they need to draw on the experience of their supervisors.

Starting in practice can be a steep learning curve with a lot of "firsts". The first client, the first ethical dilemma, the first sensation of becoming stuck and feeling out of your depth are all areas where supervision can educate and support.

However, there is one area that is implicit in the development of student counsellors, that of developing what is known as the "Internal Supervisor"—the ability to take what you have learned in supervision and apply it to self.

The term "Internal Supervisor" is attributed to British Psychoanalyst Patrick Casement, who first coined the phrase in his book, *Learning from our Mistakes*.[24]

Casement describes internal supervision as, "an internal dialogue by which analysts and therapists can monitor, moment by moment, what is happening in a session and the various options open to them, the various ways they might respond to this, and the implications for the patient in each."[25]

In other words, when working with the client, draw on your internal process to consider areas such as:

- **Transference/Counter-transference** – is this in play in the therapy room and if so, how to step out of it and work in the here and the now?

- **Boundaries** – is the client pushing boundaries? If so, how do you address this?

- **Games** – sometimes clients will "act out" in the therapy room, maybe trying to gain the attention they historically needed from a parent or caregiver.

- **Projective identification** – this is where a client may say something about others they see in themselves.

- **Legal/Ethical issues** – areas where you may need to act to stay within the law or ethical boundaries.

- **Self-care** – not to overstretch yourself and make sure you get some "me time".

- **What we learn from our clients** – this final point is crucial, as it allows you to consider how you best serve the client and tailor your responses to their unique worldview.

Developing your "Internal Supervisor" is an important personal milestone on the journey of becoming a qualified counsellor, and one that is developed in a co-created relationship with your supervisor.

This is why it is important when choosing a supervisor who is trained in the modality you are studying, that has a wide range of practice experience, and with whom you feel comfortable.

Finding the right supervisor at the beginning of your training will help you develop a robust and ethical self-supervisor.

Notes

1. Anne Thériault and Nicola Gazzola, "What Are the Sources of Feelings of Incompetence in Experienced Therapists?," *Counselling Psychology Quarterly* 19, no. 4 (2006).

2. RCH, "How to Become a Psychiatrist," *Royal College of Psychiatrists*, last modified n.d., accessed November 21, 2018. *https://www.rcpsych.ac.uk/become-a-psychiatrist/ choose-psychiatry/how-to-become-a-psychiatrist.*

3. BACP, "Training to Become a Counsellor or Psychotherapist," *British Association for Counselling and Psychotherapy,* last modified n.d., accessed November 21, 2018. *https://www. bacp.co.uk/careers/careers-in-counselling/training/.*

4. HCPC, "About Us," *Health and Care Professions Council*, last modified n.d., accessed November 21, 2018. *http://www. hpc-uk.org/aboutus/.*

5. PSA, "About Us," *Professional Standards Authority*, last modified n.d., accessed November 21, 2018. *https://www. professionalstandards.org.uk/about-us.*

6. James O. Prochaska and John C. Norcross, *Systems of Psychotherapy: A Transtheoretical Analysis*, 7th ed. (Australia; United States: Brooks/Cole Cengage Learning, 2010).

7. Greg Mulhauser, "History of Counselling & Psychotherapy," *Counselling Resource*, last modified December 20, 2014, accessed September 20, 2018. *https://counsellingresource. com/therapy/types/history/*.

8. Carl Ransom Rogers, "The Necessary and Sufficient Conditions of Therapeutic Personality Change," *Journal of Consulting Psychology* 21, no. 2 (1957).

9. Saul Rosenzweig, "Some Implicit Common Factors in Diverse Methods of Psychotherapy," *American Journal of Orthopsychiatry* 6, no. 3 (1936).

10. Colin Feltham and Windy Dryden, *Dictionary of Counselling* (London: Whurr, 1993).

11. Rogers, "The Necessary and Sufficient Conditions of Therapeutic Personality Change."

12. Keith Tudor, *The Case of the Lost Conditions. Counselling*, 1 vols., vol. 11 (2000).

13. Gerard Egan, *The Skilled Helper: A Problem-Management and Opportunity-Development Approach to Helping*, 10th ed. (Belmont, Calif.: Brooks/Cole, Cengage Learning, 2014).

14. https://www.abcawards.co.uk/wp-content/uploads/ Qualifications/1882-TOP-3__Qualification%20Guide.pdf

15. CPCAB, "Guidance to Workplace Experience – Level 4 Diploma in Therapeutic Counselling (Tc-L4)," *Counselling & Psychotherapy Central Awarding Body*, last modified n.d., accessed November 21, 2018. *http://www.cpcab.co.uk/Content/Publicdocs/ guidance_to_workplace_experience_tc-l4.pdf*.

16. Donna M. Orange, *Thinking for Clinicians: Philosophical Resources for Contemporary Psychoanalysis and the Humanistic Psychotherapies* (New York: Routledge; London: Taylor & Francis [distributor], 2010).

17. Department of Health, "What Are the Caldicott Principles?," *Information Governance Toolkit*, last modified n.d., accessed November 21, 2018. *https://www.igt.hscic.gov.uk/ Caldicott2Principles.aspx*.

18. BACP, *Ethical Framework for the Counselling Professions* (Lutterworth: British Association for Counselling and Psychotherapy, 2015).

19. Peter Jenkins, *Counselling, Psychotherapy and the Law*, 2nd ed., Professional Skills for Counsellors (Los Angeles; London: SAGE, 2007).

20. Rogers, "The Necessary and Sufficient Conditions of Therapeutic Personality Change."

21. Kavita Singh, *Counselling Skills for Managers* (Delhi: Prentice-Hall of India, 2015).

22. L. Quinn, "Working with Interpreters in Therapy," *Contemporary Psychotherapy*, last modified 2011, accessed November 23, 2018. *http://www.contemporarypsychotherapy.org/vol-3-no1-spring-2011/working-with-interpreters-in-therapy*.

23. M. Scott Peck, *The Road Less Travelled : A New Psychology of Love, Traditional Values and Spiritual Growth*, 25th anniversary ed. ed. (London: Rider, 2003).

24. Patrick Casement, *Learning from Our Mistakes : Beyond Dogma in Psychoanalysis and Psychotherapy* (Hove: Brunner-Routledge, 2002).

25. Ibid.

Bibliography

BACP. *Ethical Framework for the Counselling Professions.* Lutterworth: British Association for Counselling and Psychotherapy, 2015.

—. "Training to Become a Counsellor or Psychotherapist." *British Association for Counselling and Psychotherapy*. Last modified n.d. Accessed November 21, 2018 https://www.bacp.co.uk/careers/careers-in-counselling/training/.

—. "Types of Therapy: An a-Z of Therapeutic Approaches." *British Association for Counselling and Psychotherapy*. Last modified n.d. Accessed June 30, 2018 https://www.bacp.co.uk/about-therapy/types-of-therapy/.

Casement, Patrick. *Learning from Our Mistakes: Beyond Dogma in Psychoanalysis and Psychotherapy*. Hove: Brunner-Routledge, 2002.

CPCAB. "Guidance to Workplace Experience – Level 4 Diploma in Therapeutic Counselling (Tc-L4)." *Counselling & Psychotherapy Central Awarding Body.* Last modified n.d. Accessed November 21, 2018. *http://www.cpcab.co.uk/Content/Publicdocs/guidance_to_workplace_experience_tc-l4.pdf.*

Department for Education. *Reporting and Acting on Child Abuse and Neglect – Summary of Consultation Responses and Government Action*. London: Home Office, 2018.

Department of Health. "What Are the Caldicott Principles?" *Information Governance Toolkit*. Last modified n.d. Accessed November 21, 2018. *https://www.igt.hscic.gov.uk/Caldicott2Principles.aspx.*

Egan, Gerard. *The Skilled Helper : A Problem-Management and Opportunity-Development Approach to Helping*. 10th ed. Belmont, Calif.: Brooks/Cole, Cengage Learning, 2014.

Feltham, Colin, and Windy Dryden. *Dictionary of Counselling*. London: Whurr, 1993.

HCPC. "About Us." *Health and Care Professions Council*. Last modified n.d. Accessed November 21, 2018. *http://www.hpc-uk.org/aboutus/.*

Jenkins, Peter. *Counselling, Psychotherapy and the Law*. Professional Skills for Counsellors. 2nd ed. Los Angeles ; London: SAGE, 2007.

Mulhauser, Greg. "History of Counselling & Psychotherapy." *Counselling Resource*. Last modified December 20, 2014. Accessed September 20, 2018. *https://counsellingresource.com/therapy/types/history/.*

Orange, Donna M. *Thinking for Clinicians: Philosophical Resources for Contemporary Psychoanalysis and the Humanistic Psychotherapies*. New York: Routledge ; London : Taylor & Francis [distributor], 2010.

Peck, M. Scott. *The Road Less Travelled: A New Psychology of Love, Traditional Values and Spiritual Growth*. 25th anniversary ed. ed. London: Rider, 2003.

Prochaska, James O., and John C. Norcross. *Systems of Psychotherapy: A Transtheoretical Analysis*. 7th ed. Australia ; United States: Brooks/Cole Cengage Learning, 2010.

PSA. "About Us." *Professional Standards Authority*. Last modified n.d. Accessed November 21, 2018. *https://www. professionalstandards.org.uk/about-us*.

Quinn, L. "Working with Interpreters in Therapy." *Contemporary Psychotherapy*. Last modified 2011. Accessed November 23, 2018. *http://www.contemporarypsychotherapy.org/vol-3-no1-spring-2011/working-with-interpreters-in-therapy*.

RCH. "How to Become a Psychiatrist." *Royal College of Psychiatrists*. Last modified n.d. Accessed November 21, 2018. *https://www.rcpsych.ac.uk/become-a-psychiatrist/choose-psychiatry/how-to-become-a-psychiatrist*.

Rogers, Carl Ransom. "The Necessary and Sufficient Conditions of Therapeutic Personality Change." *Journal of Consulting Psychology* 21, no. 2 (Apr 1957): 95-103.

Rosenzweig, Saul. "Some Implicit Common Factors in Diverse Methods of Psychotherapy." *American Journal of Orthopsychiatry* 6, no. 3 (1936/07/01 1936): 412-5. doi:10.1111/j.1939-0025.1936.tb05248.x.

Singh, Kavita. *Counselling Skills for Managers*. Delhi: Prentice-Hall of India, 2015.

Thériault, Anne, and Nicola Gazzola. "What Are the Sources of Feelings of Incompetence in Experienced Therapists?". *Counselling Psychology Quarterly* 19, no. 4 (2006/12/01 2006): 313-30. doi:10.1080/09515070601090113.

Tudor, Keith. *The Case of the Lost Conditions. Counselling*. 1 vols. Vol. 11,2000.

Index

A

accepting the client *38-39*

accepting limits of competence *161*

advice-giving *44*

alcohol *40, 80, 85, 107, 162*

anxiety *32, 33, 40, 113*

Asperger syndrome *175*

assessment *16, 40, 62-63, 67, 83-87*

    clinical *151*

    notes *86-87*

    questionnaires *114*

    student counsellors *87*

B

BACP. *See British Association of Counselling and Psychotherapy*

be non-judgemental *41*

behaviourism *33*

body language *125-126, 134*

boundaries with client *91-93*

British Association of Counselling and Psychotherapy *13, 14, 19, 20, 23, 24, 29, 49, 91, 99, 108, 121, 127, 151, 161*

C

Caldicott principles *78-80*

capacity to change *173, 176*

CBT. *See Cognitive Behavioural Therapy*

Certificate in Counselling Skills

    stage of training structure *20*

Certificate of Proficiency *19*

change *85, 101, 113*

    progress *115*

    traumatic event *32*

client

    and time boundaries *3*

    boundaries *91-93*

    contracting *3*

    expectations *84*

    needs *84*

    offering a gift *ix*

    screening *83*

    sexual relationships with *91*

    signposting *85*

Client Centred Therapy *30*

Cognitive Behavioural Therapy *10, 33, 68, 114, 162*

complaints procedure *99*

conditions of worth
    boundary to help the client *174*
congruence *145*
continual professional development *24, 72, 162*
contracting *119*
counselling
    definition *30, 37*
    regulation *21-22*
    relationship *119*
    vs. psychotherapy *29-31*
counselling skills *14*
counselling training *ix, 55, 73, 145*
    introductory course *15, 20*
counsellor's proficiency *152*
counter-transference *131, 147, 194*
couples therapy *161*
courses
    accredited *24-25*
    and experience *71*
    and procedures *73*
    choosing *21*
    free *72*
CPD. See continual professional development
creating the right relationship *39*
cultural context *169*

D

Did Not Attend *179-181*
Diploma in Counselling or Psychotherapy

stage of training structure *20*
disliking/ liking the client *134*
diversity
    assessment area *84*
dress code *57*
drug rehabilitation
    and confidentiality *108*
Drug Trafficking Act 1994
    and limits to confidentiality *106*
drugs *40, 80, 85, 106, 162*
dual relationships with client *92*

E

empathy *41-42, 92*
ending stage *120-121*
environmental factors *126-127*
Equality Act 2010 *84, 126*
ethical framework *24*
Ethical Framework for the Counselling Professions 83, 91, 100, 108, 151
ethical practice *151*
ethical principles *91*
excessive questioning *44*
eye contact *43, 125-126*

F

feelings of incompetence *4, 161*
FOI. See Feelings of Incompetence
forms of contracts *100*
    therapy contract *100*
    written vs. verbal *100*

Freud, Sigmund *32-33*

G

General Data Protection Regulation
79, 98, 107, 168
good practice in reviewing *114-115*
group interview *57-58*
group supervision *64, 72*

H

Health & Care Professionals
Council *21*
titles *22*
Health and Social Work Professions
Order 2001 *22*
humanistic therapies *33-34*

I

indication of transference *133*
information sharing *80*
internal supervision process *193*
development of *194-195*

L

limits of confidentiality *38, 77, 80,*
98-99, 105-107, 108

M

making a referral *152*
Maslow, Abraham *33*
mental illness *9*

modality of therapy *97*
duration *17*

N

notes
access *98, 107*
and making referral *154*
number of sessions *38, 119-120,*
180

O

object of transference *131-132*

P

Person-Centred therapy *30, 33, 68, 84*
personality change conditions *39*
personality disorder *152*
PHD *14, 18*
phenomenology *34*
placements
and supervisions *64-65*
plan for the ending *120*
preparing for an interview *56*
process of counselling *38-41*
professional boundaries *161*
Professional Standards Authority
Accredited Register 22-23
projective identification *147, 194*
Psychoanalysis *29-33*
psychological contact *40, 84, 85,*
149
PTSD *157*

Q

qualifications
    and courses *24*
    structure of *16*

R

referral system *161*
Register of health and care
    professionals 21
research project *73*
reviewing clients' progress *113-115*
Rogers, Carl *30, 39, 42, 139*

S

self-awareness *15, 20, 87*
sexual abuse *156*
skill of attending *125-127*
SOLER *43*
stages in counselling *119-121*
supervision *92, 154, 176*
    and placements *64*
    and referrals *152*
    clinical *162*
    external *64*
    report *65*

T

taking risks in therapy *145-147*
terms and conditions of payment *99*

Terrorism Prevention and
    Investigation Measures Act 2011
    and limits to confidentiality *106*
The Money Laundering, Terrorist
    Financing and Transfer of
    Funds (Information on the
    Payer) Regulations 2017
    and limits to confidentiality *106*
therapeutic contract with the client
    101, 113-114
therapeutic process *4*
therapeutic relationship *31, 38, 39,*
    41, 119-120, 133, 134, 146, 151
Transactional Analysis *31, 33*
transference *86, 131-135*
    boundary issue *92-93*
    boundary to help the client *176*
    examples *131-132*
    power of *178*
    warning signs *133*
transference in counsellors *133*
trauma-informed practice *157-158*
traumatic event *32, 87, 158*
triggering events *86, 87, 158*
trust *32, 91, 174*
types of interview *57–59*

U

UK Counsel for Psychotherapy *23,*
    24, 49, 161
unconditional positive regard *39-41, 125, 181*

use of personal data *78-80*

V

volunteer co-coordinator *51*

volunteering *55-56, 61-63*

    advantages *56*

W

working with a third person *167-169*

working with children *67-68, 108*

Printed in Great Britain
by Amazon